THE JESUITS IN CEYLON

THE JESUITS IN CEYLON

(IN THE XVI AND XVII CENTURIES)

Fr. S. G. PERERA

GYAN

Published by

Gyan Publishing House
5, Ansari Road
Daryaganj, New Delhi-110002
Phone: 011-47034999, 9811692060
E-mail: books@gyanbooks.com

Distribution Network
gyanbooks.com
India, USA, Canada, UK, Australia, France

ISBN : 978-81-212-3639-3 (PB)
First Published, Madura, 1941

2nd Impression 2020

Printed at: Gyan Press, Delhi.

The book at your disposal is the edition of an old book originally published long back. The Text quality of this book may not be at par as compared to our other books but many readers approached us to reprint this important book so that it could satiate their hunger. We request all the readers of this book to help us to improve its quality by providing the necessary text of those pages which are not properly visible. Your valuable support in this case will be highly appreciated and acknowledged and our future readers will be benefitted immensely.

THE

JESUITS IN CEYLON

(In the XVI and XVII Centuries)

BY

Father S. G. PERERA, S. J.

DE NOBILI PRESS,
MADURA.

1941

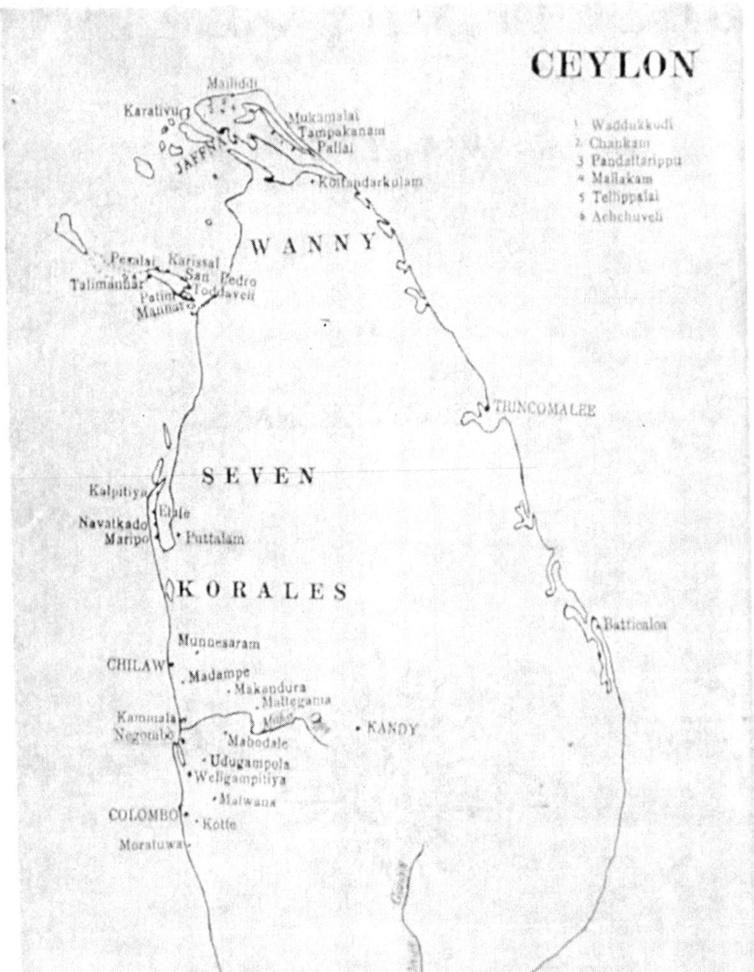
CEYLON
1 Waddukkodi
2 Chankam
3 Pandaltarippu
4 Mallakam
5 Tellippalai
6 Achchuveli
Mailiddi
Karativu
Mukamalai
Tampakanam
Pallai
JAFFNA
Kottandarkulam
WANNY
Pezalai
Karissal
San Pedro
Talimannar
Todaveli
Mannar
TRINCOMALEE
SEVEN
Kalpitiya
Navatkado
Maripo
Puttalam
KORALES
Batticaloa
Munnesaram
CHILAW
Madampe
Makandura
Mallegama
Kammala
Negombo
KANDY
Mabodale
Udugampola
Weligampitiya
Malwana
COLOMBO
Kotte
Moratuwa
GALLE

CONTENTS

FOREWORD

THE following is a short sketch of the old Jesuit Missions in Ceylon in the time of the Portuguese, written to commemorate the Fourth Centenary of the Establishment of the Society of Jesus. It is compiled mainly from manuscript sources, from original documents existing in the archives of the Society of Jesus and in the libraries of Rome, Lisbon and Colombo.

In 1916—1920 I contributed to the *Ceylon Antiquary and Literary Register* (Volumes I—VI) a series of articles on "The Jesuits in Ceylon in the XVI and XVII centuries," giving not only an account of the Jesuit Missions in Ceylon but also translations of Jesuit letters, namely letters written from Ceylon or about Ceylon by individual Jesuits to the General of the Society, to the Provincial or to their brethren abroad, annual letters, reports of missionary work, narratives of events and catalogues of the Society. Some of the letters translated purely for their interest to Ceylon history, were published in the same Review under the title of "Historical Records of the Society of Jesus."

Since then I came across quite a number of other letters relating to Ceylon both in the Society's archives and elsewhere. These I have used for the first time in this sketch, rewriting the former account and making it more complete but restricting it to the missionary endeavours of the Jesuits and omiting from it many of the references to Ceylon history contained in my first account.

S. G. PERERA, S.J.

Bishop's House,
GALLE.

27 September, 1940.

CHAPTER I

Ceylon and St. Francis Xavier

THE Society of Jesus was canonically instituted by the Bull *Regiminis Militantis Eccelesiae* issued by Paul III on 27th September, 1540; and within six months one of the original members of the new Society became deeply interested in the island of Ceylon. This was Francis Xavier, an ardent Spaniard, who from being a renowned professor of the University of Paris was transformed into 'a vessel of election to carry the name of Christ to the gentiles.' Being sent to India as Papal Legate he worked in the Fishery Coast, Molukkas and Japan, for ten years (1542—1552), and died while attempting to enter China. He was beatified in 1619, canonized in 1622, and was proclaimed the Apostle of India and the pattern of a missionary, not merely because of the phenomenal success of his apostolate, but especially because of the wise, systematic and persevering, method of missionary work he introduced and stamped on the Indian missions. [1]

By 1541 the Indian missions begun by the Portuguese missionaries appeared to King John III of Portugal to need a papal legate, and he desired to send a member of the newly founded Society of Jesus. At first the Portuguese Jesuit, Simon Rodriguez, was selected for the task,

[1] Confer the tribute paid to him by the Calvinist Minister, Philip Baldaeus, in his "Description of the Coasts of Malabar and Coromandel." Chapter XIII.

but he fell ill and Xavier was chosen in his stead. It was at Lisbon, while getting ready to set sail with the new Governor of India, Martin Affonso de Souza, that Francis Xavier first heard of Ceylon. The information he received about this island of ours made such an impression on him that on 18th March, 1541, he wrote to Ignatius of Loyola that he heard from the Governor of "an island in India inhabited by gentiles, with no Moors nor Jews, where there was great scope for the gospel, as the king of that Island himself makes no difficulty about becoming a Christian with all his people." [1]

The island thus vaguely spoken of is no other than Ceylon and the king Bhuvaneka Bahu of Kotte, with whom Martin Affonso de Souza was well acquainted. That monarch was at the time hard pressed by his brother, Mayadunna, the ruler of Sitawaka, and had been saved by the intervention of the Portuguese. He was in consequence trying his best to persuade the Portuguese to support not only him but also his favourite grandson, then an infant, whom he wished to place on the throne to the exclusion of Mayadunna who would succeed him according to the Sinhalese laws of succession. To this end Bhuvaneka Bahu had already written to the king of Portugal, and was ready to do whatever the Portuguese desired. At least so it seemed to the Governor, and so, in a sense, it was, as the king was quite willing to make any promise to gain his end. In 1541 he was even getting ready to send an embassy to Lisbon. Sri Ramaraksa Pandita, the Sinhalese ambassador, actually set out in 1542 with a casket of exquisite workmanship in which the crowning of the king's grandson by John III was depicted in ivory [2] as a symbol of the protection which

[1] See letter in G. Schurhammer, *Ceylon* 98.

[2] *Pantheon* (Bruckmann, Munchen) Dec. 1937, Jan. 1938.

Bhuvaneka Bahu desired of the Portuguese king. The Sinhalese ambassador also made king John understand, as Souza had said to St. Francis, that the king of Ceylon was willing to become a Christian and open his country to the gospel. Under that belief at all events, king John readily granted all the requests [1] of Bhuvaneka Bahu and sent some Franciscans [2] to Ceylon along with the ambassador.

Meanwhile Francis Xavier reached India and became absorbed in the work of instructing the converts of the Fishery Coast who had embraced Christianity but had so far not been properly instructed. The method hitherto followed by the missionaries was unsatisfactory, to say the least, and the instruction of the new converts had not been sufficiently attended to. In fact the priests who first came with the Portuguese were more keen on baptizing than on converting. They lived in the Portuguese settlements, ministered to the Portuguese settlers and spoke only Portuguese. When people desired to embrace Christianity the priests were satisfied with giving them a summary instruction through incompetent interpreters, after which they returned to the Portuguese settlements. The result was that the converts had, at best, only a vague appreciation of the truths of the gospel. The first care of St. Francis Xavier was therefore to remedy this defect, and he set about it with characteristic energy, writing most appealing letters to Europe for priests, more priests and better priests. All religious instruction, he said, must be given in the language of the people, and the first duty of a missionary

[1] *O Thesauro do Rey de Ceilao*, Sousa Viterbo (Lisbon 1904) pp.60-67.

[2] Friar Joao de Villa de Conde, Guardian, Friars Antonio Padram, Francisco de Monteprandone, and Siman de Coimbra were the only ones who reached Ceylon. Two others remained at Socotra. Cf. *Conquista Spiritual do Oriente* MS. Vatican Library (Lat. 7746).

was to learn the vernacular. As no missionary can be equal to the task of instructing all converts, permanent catechists must be employed in the work of evangelization; and they must be thoroughly trained for the work, and personally supervised by the missionary.

The Franciscans who had come to Ceylon, on the other hand, were doomed to disappointment. Neither would the king of Kotte become a Christian nor would he allow his subjects to do so freely. After much ado Friar Joao de Villa de Conde reported to Lisbon that the king was trying to back out of his promise. But John III to whom the promise was made by the king's ambassador, and who had granted numerous privileges to Bhuvaneka Bahu in the expectation of his becoming a Christian, wrote a letter to the Sinhalese sovereign calling upon him to keep his royal word. Francis Xavier, as papal legate, was commissioned to deliver this letter. But his intervention was of no avail. The king of Kotte whose circumstances had changed considerably since he sent the embassy, vigorously protested that he had not authorized such a promise. St. Francis realized that Bhuvaneka Bahu was no friend of Christianity in spite of the favours he had received from the king of Portugal. But two romantic episodes in Ceylon history soon stirred the heart of St. Francis to its very depths.

Bhuvaneka Bahu's attempt to place his grandson on the throne gave rise to great domestic discord. His brother Mayadunna took up arms; and his son Jugo Bandara, born to him of a junior queen, was indignant that he was passed over. Accordingly, the king had to send his ambassador once again to Goa to ask assistance against Mayadunna. To appease Jugo he begged the king of Portugal to cause the kingdoms of Jaffna and Kandy to be restored to him as they were dependencies of the kingdom of Kotte [1]; and one or the other might be given to Jugo Bandara. But this young prince had made friends with a Portuguese in Kotte named Andre de Sousa, and conceived a desire to become a Christian and seek Portuguese help. The father coming to hear of it caused him to be secretly put to death. "Those who were present say" wrote St. Francis according to his information, "that they saw a cross of fire in the heavens and that the earth opened in the form of a cross at the place where he was killed. They say also that many unbelievers saw these wonders and that many of them are disposed to be Christians. A brother of the prince seeing these marvels begged the Fathers that were there to baptize him, which they did. I had speech with this Christian prince who is proceeding to Goa to ask the help of the Governor [2]."

This second prince who gave these particulars to St. Francis, and who according to Sinhalese terminology is Jugo's 'brother,' was actually his first cousin, son of Bhuvaneka Bahu's sister. In baptism he had taken the name of Don Joao, the name of the King of Portugal. Jugo actually had a brother, a little boy; and his mother fearing for the life of her second son sent him to India along with many "gentlemen of Ceylon who became Christians there, the prince taking the name of the Infante of Portugal, Don Luis [3]." The two princes went to Goa where the Governor "received them with honour as befits the rank of the princes [4]." Soon afterwards there arrived "another Captain of the king, their father, with some ten knights and fidalgos" who went every day to the Jesuit College of St. Paul for instruction and wrote down the Christian doctrine.

[1] Bhuvaneka Bahu to the Infante Don Luis, Kotte 28 Nov. 1543.
[2] 27 Jan. 1545.
[3] Andre de Sousa, Goa, 15 Nov. 1545.
[4] Juan de Beira, Goa, 20 Nov. 1545.

The second event touched St. Francis even more closely. While he was engaged in evangelizing Travancore, the inhabitants of the little island of Mannar facing the Fishery Coast, sent him a pressing message to come to that island also and receive them into the Catholic faith. They had heard of the devotion and earnestness and personal holiness of St. Francis and of the conversion of their kinsmen in India. But St. Francis was then very busy in Travancore, for large numbers of people were moved by his tireless solicitude for their welfare, and sought instruction in Christianity. He therefore sent one of his fellow workers who soon instructed and baptized the inhabitants of Mannar. But when people embrace Christianity the king of Portugal claims to be their protector, and the king of Jaffna, within whose kingdom Mannar was situated, dreaded the consequences and sent his troops to Mannar to put to death all the new Christians who were not ready to abandon their faith. Some escaped to the mainland [1] and a large number of those who remained at Patim, men, women and children, were put to the sword [2].

St. Francis was aghast at the news. If the rajah of Jaffna were not immediately taken to task, there would be no hope for Christianity. He therefore went straight off to Cochin and thence to Goa to interview the Governor. Souza made a great show of indignation and ordered the fleet to set sail for Jaffna. St. Francis was himself to accompany the expedition, in the hope, as he himself wrote to Rome, that "God in his infinite mercy and through the devout prayers of those whom he martyred" would cause the rajah "to recognize his error and beg God for mercy and do salutary penance [3]." But such

[1] Anrrique Anrriques, 19 Dec. 1561.
[2] St. Francis, Cochin, 27 Jan. 1545.
[3] Ib.

was not to be the case. A rich Portuguese ship ran aground off Jaffna, and the Portuguese were far more concerned with recovering the precious cargo than with taking the king to task. St. Francis returned to Goa in disgust. The apathy of the Portuguese officials in regard to matters of religion greatly saddened the saint who therefore soon left for Macassar where two convert kings were asking for missionaries. He left instructions that if any members of the Society of Jesus should come from Portugal in his absence, they should be sent to Ceylon with the Sinhalese princes if they returned there. But hearing that there were already five Franciscans and two secular priests in Ceylon, he countermanded the order from Malacca.

The two Sinhalese princes meanwhile were maintained with befitting state in Goa. The Governor even made up his mind to place them on thrones in Ceylon; but the outbreak of war with the Turks prevented the expedition. On 2nd September, 1545, there arrived a new Governor in the person of Don Joao de Castro, who desired to begin negotiations over again before attempting to enthrone the princes. This took some time, and meanwhile the king of Kandy sent a message to Goa offering to become a Christian with his son and family, and even to give his daughter in marriage to Don Joao. [1] But an epidemic of small-pox broke out in Goa and carried off both the Sinhalese princes in the prime of their youth.

"On the 14th of January (1546) the Princes of Ceylon died of small-pox in this city," wrote the Viceroy to the King. "I caused them to be most honourably interred and ordered their servants to be lodged and given all they needed till they returned, when I gave them good

[1] Nunalvarez Pereira, Kandy, 12 Sept. 1545.

vessels and many gifts. They went to their country quite content. These Princes died very good Christians, and methinks that if death had not taken them away so soon, they would have rendered singular services to the Christianity that is now being set up in the Island of Ceylon [1]."

When St. Francis returned to India in 1548, he met Friar Joao de Villa de Conde from whom he learnt about the state of affairs in Ceylon. He therefore wrote a strong letter to the king of Portugal, pointing out the hostility of Bhuvaneka Bahu and still more the misdeeds of the Portuguese officials. About the former he had already written: "Would to heaven the many favours which you show the king of Ceylon had softened him not to seek to keep Jesus Christ out of his dominions!" And now he wrote about the Portuguese: "Experience has taught me that Your Highness is not powerful enough to spread the faith of Christ: You have power only to get and possess the temporal wealth of India. Pardon me for speaking so plainly, for I do so because of the love I bear you, as I fear the judgement of God that will be revealed to Your Highness at the hour of death, which none can escape, however powerful he be [2]."

[1] Don Joao de Castro to the King, 16 Dec. 1546. Schurhammer, *Ceylon*, 407.

[2] Xavier to John III, Cochin, 26 Jan. 1549. Schurhammer O. C. 533.

CHAPTER II

Father Manoel de Moraes and Brother Antonio Dyas

THE next Jesuit to visit Ceylon, and the first actually to labour in the Island, was Father Manoel de Moraes, a well known and zealous priest, of whose ability St. Francis had such a high opinion that he named him as a successor to himself. At the request of the Viceroy, Don Affonço de Noronha, Father Moraes was sent to Ceylon along with a lay brother, Antonio Dyas, in October, 1552, to try to persuade the boy king of Kotte to receive baptism. This boy had been educated by the Franciscans during the lifetime of Bhuvaneka Bahu, by whose sudden death he became king in 1551 when he was only in his teens. Father Moraes was also authorized to preach the Jubilee Indulgence in Colombo and Kotte. There are two letters, one of the Father and another of the Brother, written on different dates, giving us an account of their labours and incidentally a picture of the many disorders in Ceylon at that time [1]

Colombo was then a small Portuguese settlement, situated at the foot of the modern breakwater and surrounded by a mud wall erected in 1551. Some Portuguese adventurers lived there under a Captain recently appointed. They were, it would appear, a most unruly

[1] Antonio Dyas, Colombo, 15 Dec. 1552 cf. *Ceylon Literary Register*, III (1933—4) p. 519. See Appendix 7.

crew, leading scandalous lives, regardless of the laws of God and man. Their behaviour was a discredit to the faith which the priests had come to preach. "We saw." writes the Brother, "the way of making Christians obstructed, because the deeds which the Portuguese do here give room to the pagans to think that Our Holy Faith and Law is not so good as we preach, and they forthwith throw in our face the things which the Portuguese did and are doing. They say if our religion is good, how do we break a law so good? A great impediment to Christianity is this communication of bad Portuguese tyrants, for the pagans see how badly they live and how many violences they do to them."

The two Jesuits found hospitality with the Franciscans for a few days and received many courtesies from the Vicar of Colombo, Joao Vaz Monteiro [1]. Father Moraes called upon the Captain "to set in order a house where the sick might be treated" and where he and the Brother might lodge. This was soon done and they took up their quarters in the hastily arranged Hospital, or *Espirittal* as it was called, a word which still survives in Sinhalese. From this abode the Father began his ministry in Colombo, preaching twice on Sundays and days of obligation, while the Brother was kept busy giving catechetical instruction to the people who were in great need of it.

Father Moraes vigorously denounced from the pulpit the scandalous lives of the Portuguese and arrested attention by the very vehemence of his denunciation. Many were brought to repentence and amendment of life. When he had effected some reform in Colombo he

[1] First Vicar of Colombo (1531—1563). See "Joao Vaz Monteiro" by Father S. G. Perera, S.J. in *Ceylon Literary Register* IV (1935) 233—241.

visited Kotte, a "city all demolished and burnt, which we saw in ruins, which is a great pity to see, and I should have to write these things with tears and not with ink [1]." So great was the fame of the Father's sermons that there came to his first sermon in Kotte the Regent of the King, Sembahap Perumal, who had been Chief Chamberlain to Bhuvaneka Bahu, bringing with him another well known personage of the time who is referred to in contemporary writings and in the letter from which I am quoting as "The Black Captain," though the person so called has not yet been identified. After a few days the Brother was sent to the palace to arrange an interview with the king. The young king in his boyish curiosity asked the Brother many questions. 'What was the difference between Jesuits and Franciscans, and between them and the secular priests?' The Brother was only too pleased to give explanations; and a day was fixed for the interview. Father Moraes appeared in the palace on that day and several times subsequently and exhorted the king to become a Christian. The king was of course too young to think of coming to a decision on this or on any other subject, and everything had to be done by the Regent, who explained that the time was inopportune for such a course owing to the warfare with Mayadunna: but they would see about it when the war was over. The Regent, in fact, did himself become a Christian a few years later, and the young King followed with all his court in course of time; but the Jesuits had little to do with either event. Father Moraes broke down in health and was recalled to Goa with the Brother in 1553, to die there a few months later [2].

[1] Antonio Dyas, S.J. 1552.

[2] He died in July or August 1553, aged only 32. See Appendix 9.

CHAPTER III

The Mission of Mannar

THE first Jesuit missionaries to labour in Ceylon were the Fathers of the Fishery Coast some of whom came over to Mannar with their flocks in 1560. In that year the Viceroy, Don Constantino de Braganza, tried to carry out the long deferred orders of the sovereign of Portugal to punish the Rajah of Jaffna for the massacre of the Christians of Mannar. But in spite of initial success the attempted conquest proved an utter failure. However, on his way back to India, Braganza seized the island of Mannar, built a fortress there and sent word to the Christians of the Fishery Coast to come and settle down in "the Island of Martyrs." These Christians were at the time greatly harrassed by the neighbouring King Visvanatha, the founder of the Nayakkar dynasty of Madura, and were easily persuaded to quit their homes. Two Jesuits, Father Anrrique Anrriquez, who was then Superior of the Fishery Coast, and Father John Mesquita were to accompany them, along with a lay brother. But before the emigrants could embark an army of Vadagars appeared on the scene to prevent their prey from escaping.

The Portuguese Captain and soldiers engaged the foe while the Christians embarked in all haste and succeeded in getting safely on board, though in the hurry and precipitation a few were lost. When the Christians had all embarked the Captain ordered his men to make for the boats that were held in readiness for the purpose. The two Fathers, who had remained on shore to see the Christians safely on board, were in the boats awaiting the soldiers. Unfortunately for the Portuguese, the small boats were too heavily laden and could not make for the ship without the tide. The Vadagars thereupon attacked the boats. The Portuguese taken at a disadvantage, defended themselves as best they could, till finally they were overpowered and captured. The two Jesuits jumped into the water and tried to escape to the ships. Father Anrriquez succeeded in doing so, but his companion fell into the hands of the Vadagars. The Captain and his men finally ransomed their lives and left for Mannar with Father Anrriquez and the Brother, leaving the unfortunate Father Mesquita, of whose whereabouts they were ignorant, to his fate.

The immigrants arrived in Mannar while the Portuguese were busy erecting the fortress under the supervision of the Viceroy himself. They were received with great ceremony. The Bishop of Cochin went out to meet them preceded by a cross, and after thanking them for the service they had rendered the King and for the pleasure they had given the Viceroy, he gave them his blessing, and in a long address dwelt on the great goodness of God in bringing them to a land hallowed by the martyrs who had given their lives for the faith of Jesus Christ. Hardly had the Bishop finished his address when the Viceroy came on the scene without any formality to bid them welcome to Mannar. As the procession went past he stood by his horse and taking one of the little children of the Christians in his arms, he placed the child on the saddle and led him to the church. He appointed a Captain to the fort and placed him in charge of the pearl fishery which was thenceforth to be conducted from Mannar.

Meanwhile Father Mesquita who was held a hostage escaped from prison with the aid of a Christian boy named Miguel, and arrived with him at Mannar after sundry adventures. The Viceroy received him with transports of joy and richly rewarded the brave lad to whom the Father owed his life and who had shared the Father's captivity and perils. The care of the Christians was entrusted to the Franciscans and the Jesuits. The former immediately began the construction of a church of the Mother of God and the latter who had been the pastors of the Christians of the Fishery Coast from their first conversion continued to minister to them in Mannar.

Five long letters[1] of Father Anrriquez give us some information about the work of the Jesuits in Mannar. In the newly erected fort was Jorge de Mello de Castro, Captain of Mannar and of the Fishery. To minister to the soldiers of whom there were 150 and to the Christians of the fort, there was a Chaplain, Father Jeronimo Vaz, who lived in the fort, where he built a church, erected a Hospital and whence he looked after the Christians of Patim as well. This was a village situated half a league from the fort and inhabited, not by the immigrants from the Fishery Coast, but by the indigenous Christians of Mannar. They had abandoned their village to escape the cruelties of the Rajah of Jaffna; but when the Portuguese took Mannar they gladly returned to their former home. Their kinsmen who had not embraced Christianity all this time, also became Christians, and more than 200 souls were baptized. A church was built for them and the chaplain of the fort visited it once a week for mass and instruction. On Sundays and feast days the men went to the fort church. A lay

[1] Mannar 19 December 1561, Mannar 29 December 1562, Mannar 11 January 1564, Tuticorin 22 December 1564, Mannar 29 January 1574.

Brother, Manuel de Valladares, was appointed to help Father Vaz, and a thousand converts were added to the faith.

A little more than half a league from Patim was the chief village of the Paravar settlers hailing from all parts of the Fishery Coast except Manapad. As that was the largest single Christian community, the Fathers and Brothers made it their chief abode. At first there was only one priest, but soon there were four Jesuits; two priests and two lay brothers. A little further three large churches were built for immigrants, two for the Paravars and one for the Kadeiars, and permission was obtained for Father Diego de Soveral [1] to say two masses on Sundays and feast-days as the Superior Father Anrriquez was subject to physical infirmities resulting from a cruel captivity among the Vadagars. Besides the three large churches several smaller ones were built, one in each village, and the children assembled there for regular instruction and a sermon by one of the Brothers. During the week mass was said once in every church by the chaplain of the fort or by Father Soveral. Three leagues from this residence there was a church, at Talemanar, begun originally by the Franciscans but handed over to the secular priests of Cochin. There also were some indigenous Christians as well as the immigrants from Manapad. This church was served at this time by a secular priest placed there by the Bishop of Cochin. As he was not always there Father Soveral or another went every fourth Sunday to say mass and preach.

Besides the hospital in the fort, which was mostly, though not solely, for the Portuguese troops, another

[1] Born 1524, entered the Society 1546, set out for India 1554; 1555 Cochin, 1559 Cape Comorin, 1560 Mannar; died in a wreck off Nagapatam, 1585.

hospital was set up in the island at the cost of the Christians. This hospital was intended, not for the Christians only, but for others as well. "It is a work of great edification to the Catholics as well as to unbelievers. The latter build many things; but hospitals they have not." Many Christians served in the hospital out of devotion, and all contributed freely for its upkeep. Three young soldiers of the fort felt called to serve God and spent some time in nursing the sick in the hospital, and eventually entered religious orders, one becoming a Franciscan, having been of that Order before, and the other two, Jesuits [1].

Father Anrriquez began in Mannar another apostolate that had borne great fruit in Punnaikayal, namely discussions with non-Christians. Whenever an outsider came to Mannar the Christians spoke to him of God and Christianity, and if he showed interest he was brought to the Residence for friendly discussion with the Fathers. These discussions took place in the open and proved very useful, not only to unbelievers "but even to Christians, who thereby improve in the knowledge of their faith." On one occasion, it is recorded, a Yogi who came to Mannar attended one of these discussions. In this discussion not only Father Anrriquez but even some Christians took part, for there were in Mannar "some wise, honourable and elderly, persons elected by the Pattankattis before the Captain of the fort to be judges of the people in their disputes." One of these judges intervened when the Yogi answered the priest. This man brought good reason to show that the Yogi was not correct in his statement of the method of obtaining pardon

[1] One was Goncalo Fernandez, a soldier who came with Braganza. Born in 1541, he left the army at Mannar in 1561, entered the Society in 1562, laboured 40 years in the Fishery Coast and died at Tuticorin 6 April, 1621, and was buried by the side of Father Anrriquez.

for one's sins. This reasoning is said to have made a great impression on another unbelieving 'senhor' of the audience. Many conversions were made in this way.

Though Father Anrriquez was in poor health he was remarkably active in missionary work, especially by means of his writings, at which he spent a great part of the night when his infirmities would not let him sleep. His great grief was that there were not enough priests fully versed in Tamil. He had written to the Provincial to send to Mannar a Tamil priest who had just been ordained at Cochin, hoping to have the assistance of this priest not only in apostolic work but also in the revision of the Catechism for the people and a Grammar and Vocabulary for the Missionaries which he was composing. He was also eager to revise a prose Catechism written in a form to be chanted and some Canticles, both composed by a Tamil Christian of Colombo under the inspiration of the Franciscan friar Joao de Villa de Conde, Guardian of the Franciscans in Ceylon. This man sent his composition to the Pattankattins and chief man of Mannar who were so pleased with it that they paid fifty cruzados[1] for a copy and had it chanted in the churches of Mannar by young men with good voices. This chant catechism as well as the canticles Father Anrriquez was very eager to print for general use. But before doing so he naturally wished to see them purified of errors, and wrote to Friar Joam to send to Mannar "a priest of the country" who was in Colombo, and "who knows Latin well and has some knowledge of the making of canticles." This priest came to Mannar and helped the veteran missionary in his literary as well as his missionary work. He was, it is

[1] A gold coin of Portugal worth 400 reis, later struck in silver. The word was used to devote a sum of 400 reis, roughly equivalent to one rupee.

said, greatly edified by the piety of the Catholics of Mannar and went so far as to say that they were "better than those of Ceylon," that is, of the kingdom of Kotte.

Father Anrriquez then wrote to his Provincial about printing these literary works. Printing was a new art at the time, and no Tamil type had as yet been cast. A lay brother[1] in Cochin was acquainted with printing and was trying to cast type; but as he fell severely ill at the time, Father Anrriquez even urged the Provincial to get out from Portugal another Brother or a good workman so as to be able to print books in Tamil "as well for the instruction of the Christians as to bring unbelievers to a recognition of their errors and to print the Vocabulary and Grammar" for the use of missionaries. This entreaty of the hard worked Superior of Mannar bore fruit in due course, and resulted in the establishment of the first Tamil press[2] and the publication of Tamil books.

Father Anrriquez was one of the first Jesuits, and probably the first European, to master the intricacies of Tamil grammar. He began the study of the language on the recommendation of St. Francis Xavier and with the encouragement of St. Ignatius of Loyola. He soon acquired the language so thoroughly that in 1566 he became the head of the Tamil University set up at Punnaikayal where he had as his assistant Brother Pero Luis,[3] a

[1] Br. Juan de Bustamante *alias* Goncalvez, a Spaniard, born at Valencia, entered the Society in 1555, arrived in India 1556, and set up a printing press.

[2] Joao de Faria, born 1539, entered the Society 1562, arrived in Goa 1572. Cast Tamil type at Punnaikayal in 1578. Died 1581.

[3] A Brahmin, born at Quilon 1532, converted in 1547, served the Missionaries as interpreter, learnt Latin under Fr. N. Lanci'otti, entered the Society in 1562, the first Indian Jesuit, and was ordained priest in 1574, according to data given by himself in a letter of 2 Jan. 1589. Died, Cape Comorin 1596.

Brahamin convert of his, the first Indian to be received into the Society of Jesus. Brother Pero Luis was at Mannar for a time with Father Anrriquez. It was originally intended to found this Tamil College at Mannar and the Bishop encouraged the scheme, chose a site and even donated some money. But eventually Punnaikayal was found to be more suitable.

Under the direction and example of Father Anrriquez three lay brothers of Mannar, Francisco Durao [1], Manoel de Barros and Estevao de Goes, learnt Tamil with great diligence and were in consequence sent to Cochin to study for the priesthood. Barros had had a classical education in his youth and was therefore able to go through his priestly studies speedily. He knew Tamil not only for general use in conversation, but sufficiently well to read and write. Ordained in March 1563 he returned to work in Mannar. Very soon the Jesuits of Mannar became known for their facility in the use of the language of the country, for under the inspiration of the Superior they decided to speak only Tamil even among themselves, each one giving himself a penance if ever he spoke Portuguese. The presence of Brother Pero Luis was a great help in this matter, though he himself was able to speak Portuguese and wrote Father Anrriquez' letters to Europe, as the old priest wrote a very erratic hand. In this way the mission of Mannar made great progress and the Christians of the Island of Martyrs were held up as a model to others. In 1563 Father Anrriquez was able to write to his brethren in Europe that though he had been sixteen years with these Christians, he never had such success as at Mannar in that year.

[1] Born in the Diocese of Evora in 1528, set out for India 1551 Fishery Coast 1558, Ordained priest 1571 and died at Quilon 7 June 1612, aged 84, in the Society 62, of which 50 were spent on the Fishery Coast.

In the following year, however, the mission had to face a severe trial, for a pestilence broke out and carried off 4,000 persons, which was nearly half the immigrants. The Fathers did their best to relieve the suffering and assisted the patients to the end with great devotion and charity, even going the length of raising loans to help the needy. This dread visitation alarmed the Paravars. War and famine they were accustomed to in the Fishery Coast, but pestilence they dreaded, and therefore decided to return to their mother country. Some of the Jesuits returned with them, while a few remained behind to minister to those who preferred to stay and to the Catholics of the island. Thenceforth the mission of Mannar was to all practical purposes only a Residence of the mission of the Fishery Coast. There were always at least two priests, occasionally three, and one lay brother, all of whom were able to speak Tamil.

In 1566 when the Bishop of Cochin paid his pastoral visit there were few Jesuits in Mannar. The prelate was accompanied by a Jesuit, Father Melchior Nunez, who records that there were only two Fathers in Mannar at the time, one in the fort and the other in charge of the Christians. The Bishop was not at all pleased to see so few missionaries in so large a field and did not disguise his displeasure then, nor fail to charge the Jesuits with it afterwards. But the paucity of labourers was due to the return of the immigrants to India where too they had to be ministered to.

In 1572 there were two priests, one in the fort and the other in charge of the Christian villages. In the larger of these villages, the pestilence had done its worst, but when the majority of the immigrants returned to the Coast the rest set up a Misericordia, namely a charitable confraternity, to look after the hospital. They collected weekly subscriptions and kept up the institution with great zeal. Two free hospitals in one small island was considered a triumph of Christian charity. The smaller village was generally served by the Father stationed in the fort. A lay brother was also stationed in Mannar to help the missionaries and to learn Tamil. The number of adult baptisms in 1572 was 257, including in that number two chiefs who came from the mainland with their families and settled down in Mannar.

In 1574 Father Anrriquez came on a visit to Mannar to meet the Bishop of Cochin. At the request of the Captain he sent pressing letters to Goa to ask for reinforcements for Mannar as the island was threatened both by the Malabars and by Rajasinha of Sitawaka. But soon there came a new Captain of Mannar who gave great trouble to the people by his exactions. The Jesuits took up the cause of the oppressed people so wholeheartedly that their lives were no longer safe and they fled to the Christian villages. There they were met by Father Alexander Valignanì, Visitator of the Missions, who being unable to remedy the evil, withdrew the Chaplain from the fort and appointed him permanently to work among the Christians. There they did good work, for in 1583 we learn that there were no less than six hundred converts. "It is not an easy matter for so few priests to minister to so large a flock, but the people are very pious and very generous. Recently they gave 500 *aurei*[1] for the relief of the poor and also contributed to the support of the two hospitals in the Fishery Coast."

Among the Christians of Mannar were a number of royal refugees from Kandy. When Rajasinha invaded the Kingdom of Kandy, its king, Karalliyadde Bandara,

[1] "Gold coins", obviously *cruzados,* that is Rupees. Cf. n. 1, p. 17.

had to flee with his family and court. His family included a nephew, Yamasingha, and a little daughter named Dona Catherina. The king and queen who were Christians died of small-pox; and Yamasingha, who became Don Philip in baptism, was brought up by the Franciscans who took him to Goa. An attempt was soon made to place Don Philip on the throne of Kandy. From Mannar he was taken to the hill country and enthroned; but one of his followers, Konappu Bandara, who had taken the name of Don Juan of Austria in baptism, caused his death and seized the throne. Thereupon his son, a boy named Don Joao, was proclaimed King but he had to be removed to Mannar, whence he was taken to Goa and afterwards to Lisbon where he became a priest[1].

Another expedition was got up in 1594 to recover Kandy for the princess Dona Catherina the only surviving heir to the Kandyan throne who was being brought up in Mannar. The Jesuit Fathers had little to do with these events except as spectators; but Pedro Lopes de Souza who led this second expedition took with him a Jesuit Father of the Fishery Coast as chaplain, and his presence in Colombo after the rout of Souza, led to the establishment of the Ceylon Mission of the Society of Jesus.

[1] Don Joao died in Lisbon on 1st April 1642 aged 64, and was buried in the church which he had built at Telheiras, a suburb of Lisbon.

CHAPTER IV

Fathers Antonio Schipano and Manoel de Viega in Colombo

THOUGH some members of the Society of Jesus visited Colombo after the departure of Father Moraes, no one remained long or undertook any ministry in the city till Father Antonio Schipano, a Neapolitan Jesuit, missionary of the Fishery Coast, arrived at Colombo in 1594 after a short captivity in Kandy. He had been especially invited to accompany Pedro Lopes de Souza and had gone from Mannar as military chaplain in the expedition to Kandy to enthrone Dona Catherina. Having reduced the low country to the obedience of the former boy-king, now "Don Joao Periya Pandar, by the Grace of God, King of Ceylon"[1] who had nominated the King of Portugal as heir to the throne of Kotte, the Portuguese tried to enthrone in Kandy their ward, the young Kandyan princess, who was the undoubted heir to the throne of Kandy and had been bred a Catholic at Mannar from her childhood. That ill-fated expedition actually succeeded in entering Kandy and ousting the usurper, Konappu Bandara *alias* Don Juan of Austria, the apostate. But the success was short-lived, for though the Kandyans flocked eagerly to the banner of their young queen, they were soon repelled

[1] Thus he called himself in a letter to Pope Gregory XIII. See *Ceylon Antiquary*. VI 27–32 and *Ceylon Library Register* IV, 425, "Letter of Don Joao Peria Pandar" by Fr. S. G. Perera, S.J.

by the domineering attitude of the Portuguese. The wily Konappu profited by the circumstance and winning the people to his support forced the Portuguese to retreat, routed them completely at Gannoruwa and seized the princess. Father Schipano says that he was for a long time unhurt by the shower of arrows that fell around him. At last, however, while he was hearing the confession of a dying Captain he was wounded, though not severely, and taken captive. Though Konappu was very cruel in his triumph, he appears to have saved the Father's life. "The enemy king" says the Father, "though an apostate from our holy faith, treated me with kindness and sent me to Colombo as his ambassador to treat of peace." [1] A truce was made, and they were awaiting the reply of the Viceroy in December, 1594 when Father Schipano wrote to Rome.

His presence in Colombo, in the monastery of the Franciscans, created a situation of great delicacy. The people of Colombo as well as the new General, were eager to secure the ministrations of the members of the Society of Jesus, and made no secret of it. This was promptly opposed by the Franciscans, for one of the greatest impediments to the evangelization of mission countries is the inevitable human tendency to introduce personal and private and national considerations even in that work. The Sovereign Pontiff had to intervene to prevent the Catholic Missions from being identified with Portuguese conquests, by founding the Congregation of the Propaganda Fide to take over the direction of missions from the king of Portugal, who was seeking to restrict missionary work to his subjects and to those who would own allegiance to him and consent to work under his directions and sail in his ships from Lisbon. Simi-

[1] Antonio Schipano, S.J., to the General of the Society, Colombo 13 Dec. 1594.

larly the Religious Orders also showed a most undesirable tendency to what may be called ecclesiastical monopoly, endeavouring to prevent those of another Order from working in the field in which one Order was already engaged.

The Franciscans in Ceylon were the first missionaries in this island and had borne the heat of the day and the burden thereof for many years. Several friars had lost their lives in the wars of Ceylon,[1] and in return for such services they expected to prevent any other Religious Order from coming to Ceylon for missionary work, although the field was vast, and many people who had desired to embrace Christianity had neither been instructed nor baptized for want of missionaries capable of doing such work. Father Schipano was able to speak and preach in two Indian vernaculars one of which was Tamil, which was the current speech in many districts in Ceylon. He was, moreover, very acceptable to the soldiers and the Portuguese residents of Colombo. They, therefore, began to take steps to secure his remaining among them. They wrote to the Jesuit Provincial in India, and fearing that the Bishop of Cochin, who was a Franciscan and in whose diocese Ceylon lay, would oppose it, the people even wrote to the King of Portugal and to the Pope. The Franciscans meanwhile obtained a number of certificates from public officials testifying to their sufficiency for Ceylon.

This caused great perplexity to Father Schipano who was even informed by the General that orders would be given forbiding any ship to take him from Ceylon. Accordingly, Father Schipano wrote two letters, one on the 9th and the other on the 13th of December,

[1] *Conquista Spiritual do Oriente* Ms. Ch. 19 'of the many Friars Minor put to death on diverse occasions in Ceylon.'

1594, exposing the state of affairs in Colombo. The first letter was sent by the hands of a Venetian who was an officer on board a ship returning to Europe. It appears that the people of Colombo were so keen on having some Jesuits in the city that they had made arrangements, as it was within their power, to hand over the chapel of the Misericordia to the Society of Jesus. The Misericordia was a confraternity for poor relief and had a chapel and the administration was in the hands of *mordomos* or wardens. It seemed to them that the Misericordia was a fit abode for the Jesuits at whose instance the first hospital was set up in Colombo. But in spite of all attempts the Provincial recalled Father Schipano[1] to India after he had been ten months in the Island.

Shortly after the flight of Father Schipano from Colombo a ship of Malacca put into the harbour bearing on board another Jesuit Father, Manoel de Veiga. When he came on shore the General and the people of Colombo entreated him to remain in the city "saying that they would write to Goa and obtain permission from the Father Provincial."[2] But Father Veiga knew of the opposition of the friars and would not consent; whereupon "they put him in the casa da Misericordia, to keep him in an honourable and affectionate confinement until the ship set sail." The Father knew that there was a movement in the Society to divide the Jesuit missions in India into two Provinces, as the interests of Southern India, the languages and people and needs, were different from those of the North. As a matter of fact a decision had already been taken and Father Veiga was himself destined to be the first head of the new Province. He

[1] Antonio Schipano, born 1540 at Catanzzarro, Naples, entered the Society in 1559, set out for India in 1585; Ceylon 1594, Rector of Cochin 1602-1607, Goa 1610, Died 8 Dec. 1624.

[2] Jeronimo Gomez, 14 Jan. 1603.

therefore escaped the entreaties and continued his voyage. But the earnestness of the people and the needs of the country must have made an impression on him, for it was he who eventually accepted the invitation of the Bishop of Cochin to begin a Jesuit mission in Ceylon, and despatched the first batch of Jesuits in 1602.

CHAPTER V

The Jesuit Mission in Ceylon

THE Ceylon Mission of the Society of Jesus, begun in 1602, was the outcome of an agitation by the people of Colombo. The foremost agitator was the Captain-General of Ceylon, Don Jeronimo de Azevedo, whose half-brother, Ignatius de Azevedo, was a Jesuit and a distinguished missionary of Brazil, put to death along with thirty nine others, in hatred of the faith on 5 July, 1570. His eagerness to introduce the Jesuits into the country of which he was the military governor, was doubtless greatly influenced by his desire to honour the Religious Order to which his brother had belonged. But the chief reason why the Portuguese residents of Colombo were so bent on having a house of the Jesuits in Colombo, was that there was no secondary school in the city for the education of their children. The ultimate reason for sending the Jesuits to Ceylon, however, was neither the request of Azevedo nor the entreaties of the people, but the appeal of the diocesan bishop. The kingdom of Kotte had become a Portuguese province by virtue of a bequest of the last king, Don Joao Periya Pandar who died in 1597. The king of Portugal who was now sovereign of Kotte became alive to the responsibility of evangelizing the country. Evangelical labourers were few in Ceylon, and there were many parts of the country, such as, for instance, the whole stretch of land to the north of Colombo inhabited by people who were willing and ready to be Christians, that had not yet been evangelized for want of missioners. Hence it was felt to be high time to end the monopoly that the Franciscans claimed for themselves. Accordingly, the King of Portugal sent orders to the Viceroy of India and to the Archbishop of Goa to take counsel together and send more missionaries to Ceylon. But before these royal despatches were actually received in India, Dom Frey Andreas de Santa Maria, Bishop of Cochin and diocesan of Ceylon, visited the island and became aware of the possibilities in Ceylon and the dearth of missionaries. He knew that the Fathers of the Society were most active in mission work, and that following the example of St. Francis Xavier and the instructions of St. Ignatius, they were most zealous in instructing the converts, taking great pains to learn the languages of the country. He was himself a Franciscan, but considered it his duty in conscience to secure more missionaries for Ceylon than the Order of St. Francis provided for the island. He knew that his religious brethren had obtained from Cardinal Alberto in the name of the King of Portugal an order forbidding other religious to preach the gospel in Ceylon. When he was confronted with this document he declared that it was not the king of Portugal but the diocesan Bishop who would have to answer for it on judgment day. Moreover, he had been so greatly impressed by the prospects of the gospel in Ceylon that he was quite ready to give up the bishopric of Cochin and become Bishop of Ceylon.[1] On his return to India therefore, he prevailed upon the Viceroy and the Archbishop to send Jesuit missionaries to Ceylon. At this very time the Society of Jesus was so widely engaged in missionary work in India that its Colleges and missions had to be grouped under two

[1] Manoel de Viega, Cochin 11 January, 1601.

Provincial superiors, one resident at Goa in charge of the Northern Province, or the Province of Goa, and the other at Cochin in charge of the Southern or the Malabar Province. It was this latter Province of Malabar of which Father Viega was Vice-Provincial, that was called upon to undertake a Mission in Ceylon.

Four Jesuits arrived in Colombo in April, 1602, with letters patent bearing date the 27th February, 1602, and empowering them to preach the gospel in Ceylon. The party was led by Father Diego da Cunha, an experienced missionary of the Fishery Coast and member of the illustrious Portuguese family of the Guzmans.[1] With him were two priests, Octavio Lombardo[2] an Italian, Christopher Joam,[3] a Portuguese, and a scholastic named Pedro Euticio.[4] They were soon followed by two others, Father Balthazar Garcia[5] and a lay-brother, Andreas Vas.[6] They were received with open arms and great demonstrations by the populace of Colombo. The General was foremost in his attentions. He took them under his personal protection, maintained them at his private cost, bought them a house for two thousand *pardaos*[7] and undertook to found a College of the Society

[1] Born 1539, entered the Society 1561, Fishery Coast 1581, Rector, Tuticorin 1601, Colombo 1602—1604, Mannar 1605—6, Rector of the Fishery Coast 1608—1611. Died, Cochin 1611.

[2] He set out for India 1592, Colombo 1602—4, then Manapad, Virapandiyapatam, 1611 returned to Europe.

[3] Born at Covilha 1552, came to India 1599, Colombo 1602, 1606 Superior, 1608 Rector, 1610 Cochin, Rector there, St. Paul's Goa, died Goa, 25 May 1624.

[4] A Portuguese, 1602 Puttalam, 1604 Chilaw, 1606 Moratuwa and Malwana. Died in 1608 of fever contracted in the Seven Korales.

[5] Born at Barcellis 1573, entered the Society 1599, arrived in India 1601, 1602 Colombo, 1605 Kammala, 1610—15 Molukkas, 1615 returned to Colombo and died there.

[6] Afterwards expelled from the Society.

[7] *Pardao*, originally *pratapa* or Pagoda, applied to various coins of about the same value, (360 *reis*) also called *Zerafim*, roughly equivalent to one Rupee.

in Colombo. The Franciscans, however, were indignant and challenged the right of the ecclesiastical and civil authorities to override the royal decree granting them the exclusive right of evangelization in Ceylon. After some unseemly opposition in Ceylon they carried their grievance to Goa. The newcomers meanwhile remained inactive and the prudent superior set his men the task of learning Sinhalese. Tamil they already knew.

Fortunately the Bishop of Cochin again arrived in the Island at this juncture and wished to take the responsibility on himself; but the representatives of the Church and state declared juridically that the King's former *alvara* was revoked by his subsequent instructions; and the Franciscans acquiesced for the while, sending their protests to Rome and Lisbon. The Bishop thereupon made a division of the island for purposes of evangelization. The Franciscans were to remain in the parts in which they had already built churches, and the rest of the island not yet evangelized was declared the missionary field of the Society of Jesus. The island was thus divided into two, a northern part from the Maha Oya upwards, in charge of the Jesuits, and a southern part, from the Maha Oya downwards, in charge of the Franciscans. The Jesuit district comprised what is now the Dioceses of Chilaw, Jaffna and Trincomalee, of which only the territory of Chilaw, now the North-Western Province, then called the disawa of the Seven Korales, was at the time accessible to the gospel. The field of the Franciscans was principally the disawa of Matara, extending from Colombo to the Walawe. Later on, when other Religious Orders came to work in Ceylon, the disawa of Sofragam or Sabaragamuwa was assigned to the Augustinians and the Four Korales to the Dominicans. The Franciscans, however, retained the administration of all churches erected by them even in the missionary domain of the others; the Jesuits likewise erected churches in the villages of which the revenues were given to them for their maintenance, though situated in the province of the other Orders. In the city of Colombo all the Religious Orders had churches and institutions, but the parish churches were in charge of secular priests appointed by the Bishop of Cochin.

CHAPTER VI

The College of Colombo

IT was principally to have the benefit of a secondary education for their children that the people of Colombo were so eager for members of the Society of Jesus. The first thing, therefore, that the Jesuits did in Ceylon was to open a school in Colombo. It was at first a very unpretentious institution, practically only an elementary school, begun in an ordinary dwelling house within the Fort purchased for them by Azevedo and hurriedly arranged to serve as a school and a residence for the Fathers. In it the boys were taught to read, write, cipher and sing. Very soon classes began to be given in Latin to students who desired a classical education. The staff consisted of two Fathers and a lay-brother. Even so "the people were extremely grateful to us for providing their children with a sound education in letters and morals and other accomplishments, a benefit they hitherto lacked."[1]

The scholars were chiefly the sons of the Portuguese residents in Ceylon with a few Sinhalese boys of the better class. As all the students of the College are spoken of as *Ceilanenses*, that is 'Ceylonese' in the sense that they were children born in Ceylon, it cannot be determined how many or what percentage of them were Portuguese by blood, and how many, people of the country. The only schoolboys of whom any particular

[1] Christopher Joam, 1 Dec. 1609.

mention is made are the sons of Sinhalese princes of whom some are mentioned at various times as attending the College. The sons of the Princes of Uva and of the Seven Korales were educated in the Jesuit College, besides sons of some petty chiefs. The number of scholars is mentioned only once, and it was 150, which we may take as the average number.

In 1605 the College was shifted to a more suitable site in a conspicuous locality, and new buildings were set up with classrooms, dormitories, a residence for the Fathers and a church. The new site is what is now the junction between the Main Street and Front Street Pettah, over against the present Consistory buildings, which occupy the site of the Town Hall or Chamber of Colombo in Portuguese times. In front was an open space, once called the 'Raket Court' now the Chalmers Granaries. Hard by the College was the town residence of the Captain-General, Don Jeronimo de Azevedo. He was the founder of the College, and he not only bought the property and maintained the Fathers at his cost for some time, but actually endowed the College with the revenues of certain villages. When he was appointed Viceroy of India he even gave the College his furniture.

Jesuit Colleges do not charge fees for tuition, and colleges can only exist when some generous benefactor gives them the means to maintain a staff. The endowment of the College of Colombo was not only intended to maintain the Fathers engaged in teaching, but also those who were being prepared there for mission work. When they are actually engaged in that work they are maintained by the State, which gave a subsistence of ten *pardaos* a month to each missionary. [1]

[1] *Documentos Remettidos da India* IV, 33.

Besides this endowment the College possessed "some small thatched houses that were given by some devout persons" which "yielded an annual income of fifty *pardaos*, more or less." A generous Portuguese widow of Colombo, named Mercia Roiz "made a donation to the College, *inter vivos*, of 8664 *pardaos*, which were already yielding interest, on condition that in her life time 200 *parduos* were to be drawn annually for her support, 160 *pardaos* for the Casa da Misericordia, of which 100 *pardaos* were to be given as dowry to an orphan and the other 60 to the poor.

Moreover she made this donation to the College on the condition that it should carry out whatever she had laid down in her will, and that the remainder of the interest be spent on the new church; and when it was finished, the money be left to yield interest till the capital and the interest together was enough to support twenty religious. In 1617, however, she made another document ratifying the gift and allowing the money to be used for buying property. Unfortunately 2560 *pardaos* were lost at sea, but when her life interest ceased the capital would give the college 400 *pardaos* a year.[1] All these endowments enabled the college to maintain ten or twelve persons.

The staff of the College consisted of a Rector, who was at the same time the religious Superior of the missionaries, a minister, teachers, prefects and a spiritual Father. There were also in the College one or more Fathers for preaching, hearing confessions and administering the sacraments. Originally there were only three Jesuits in the College, but the number gradually increased to five and rose occasionally even to twelve. Some

[1] Foundation and Origin of the College of Colombo, MS. in the Archives, S.J.

members of the Society not yet priests were educated in the College. Four students of the College are known to have joined the Society, one of whom wrote the first Sinhalese Grammar written in a European tongue.

In course of time the College grew to be a fairly large educational institution with three distinct departments of study. The highest was a course of lectures in moral philosophy and theology, introduced at the request of the Bishop of Cochin and meant chiefly for ecclesiastical students. The College proper was a Secondary school teaching the Humanities and Rhetoric according to the Ratio Studiorum of the Jesuits. The third division was an elementary school teaching the rudiments. Tavernier has something to say about the intelligence of the students of this College, for according to him the Jesuits "found that the youth of Ceylon were so quick and intelligent that they learnt in six months more Latin, philosophy and other sciences than Eurepeans acquire in a year and they questioned the Fathers with such subtility and so deeply that they were amazed."[1] In proof of his statement Tavernier adduced the case of Alagiyawanna who acquired Latin very thoroughly in six months and set himself to read the New Testament. We may therefore suppose that the Frenchman's compliment referred to the Sinhalese students of the College.

To the College was attached a Church facing the Rua Direita which is now represented by the Main Street of the modern Pettah. Between the College and the Church was the residence of the Fathers. The first church was a small building, but on Whit Sunday 1613 the foundation was laid for a new church in Corinthian style with an imposing facade. "Though we are badly

[1] Jean-Baptiste Tavernier, *Travels*. Ball's Translation II 148.

off for means, we hope with the help of God to bring it to a speedy conclusion." When completed it was expected to be "if not the best in the whole of India, at least the second best." The Church was dedicated to the Purification of the Blessed Virgin and on the feast of the church the College boys regularly staged a dramatic performance. "The stage equipment," it is said, is "far from ordinary and the acting greatly appreciated."

The progress of the College called for new buildings but it was decided to finish the Church before beginning the new enterprise. Soon, however, both the College and the mission were to go through a severe tribulation. A revolt caused the devastation of the mission, and the College had to face the calamity of having its endowment withdrawn by the civil authority.

CHAPTER VII

The Beginning of the Mission

IT was only towards the end of 1602 that the Jesuits in Colombo were able to begin their mission work in earnest. Up to that time the Superior very wisely set his companions the task of learning Sinhalese. He also opened a school and arranged the small houses bought for them to serve as a residence for the Fathers, a chapel and a school. The first mass in this new chapel was said by the Bishop of Cochin on 30th November which was the feast of his name-saint. The General was present and entertained the prelate and the Fathers to a dinner supplied by him in the Jesuit house. In the evening Colombo witnessed for the first time a dramatic performance got up for the occasion by the scholars of the new school. The chief ministry of the Fathers in the beginning was giving religious instruction to the people, a thing that had so far been badly neglected. They also visited the prison and the hospital, and preached on Sundays and feast-days in the parish church.

After the Epiphany of 1603 two members of the Society set out for their mission field and erected at Weligampitiya, Kammala, Madampe, Chilaw and Puttalam, temporary churches of very simple construction. Another Father went at the General's request to the Seven Korales with the troops of Mudaliar Dom Fernando Samarakoon, while a fourth took up residence with the General at his official head-quarters at Malwana. This last was not to be a missionary there, for it was in the district of the Franciscans, but a kind of chaplain to Azevedo, and he catechized the General's household and learnt Sinhalese, for which, it is said, the place was especially suited. He was also directed to keep a record of events in the island and to investigate its history and antiquities.

The mission field of the Jesuits proved to be white unto harvest. The people living on the sea board of Ceylon had made up their mind long ago to embrace Christianity, but had so far had no opportunity of doing so. The Jesuit missionaries were able to speak Tamil, which was the language currently spoken in that part of the Island. Accoidingly their success was great. In Chilaw where there were only seven Christians when the Fathers arrived, the whole populace, estimated at 5,000, headed by the *Pattankattis* or chief men, placed themselves under instruction. Effective religious instuction was a strong point of the Jesuit missionary method. From the time of St. Francis Xavier, whose first preoccupation in India was the instruction of converts, the Jesuits insisted on a thorough and systematic instruction of their neophytes.

But unfortunately there broke out in Ceylon a widespread revolt against Portuguese rule. The kingdom of Kotte had only recently passed under the sovereignty of the King of Portugal on the death of the natural king, Don Joao Periyapandar, who had bequeathed his Crown by will to the King of Portugal But the short experience of Portuguese rule was already beginning to make it very galling. Not content with possessing the low country, Azevedo set his heart on reducing the kingdom of Kandy by ousting Konappu Bandara *alias* Wimaladharma Suriya, who had been brought up among the Portuguese, had fought for them in Colombo, lived in Goa and married a Portuguese wife, but subsequently profitting by an opportunity, usurped the throne of Kandy, turned against his whilom friends and renounced the Christian faith. To oust this renegade was the hope and desire and effort of every Portuguese of that time.

Early in 1603 Azevedo planned an expedition to Kandy for the purpose. In his army were numbers of Sinhalese troops who had been accustomed to fight their own countrymen, the Kandyans, as long as the Portuguese were fighting for Don Joao, their natural king; but it proved to be a fatal mistake to expect them to fight for the aggrandizement of Portugal. Azevedo's army successfully stormed Balana, the lofty pass leading to Kandy. Thereupon, says the Jesuit Superior of Colombo, who accompanied the expedition, "our men were so proud of this entry that they thought everything was secure: the lascarins and their captains and chiefs so dispirited and disheartened, that even those who went to battle with us, remained faithful only in appearance, thinking that the Portuguese would thenceforth be absolute masters of the island and make no account of them. Many, moreover, went with us against their will. Thus the lascarins and the camp followers, more than three thousand in all, resolved to desert the Portuguese in a body at the top of the hill.

They then came down into the low country, killing and plundering all the Portuguese and the Christians they met. As the forts at the foot of the mountains were ill-provided with men and munitions, they were all taken and set on fire; and in these various encounters they killed more than a hundred Portuguese. As they gave out that the General and all the Portuguese were killed, the people were easily moved to rise in revolt with great joy and eagerness, for it seemed to them that they were rid of the yoke and subjection of the Portuguese, which, in truth, is very great, considering the violence and hardship they had to suffer.

Seeing the state of affairs, the General led his army down the hill with great difficulty and lost some men, both in the descent and on the way, which lay through thick forests for a distance of twenty five leagues. This took fifteen days as the whole island had risen in revolt. While our men were retiring, the enemy gained strength and obstructing the ways, and erecting many stockades, they strongly opposed the retreat." [1]

The two Fathers who accompained the expedition Diego da Cunha and Octavio Lombardo "had no lack of hardships; for as the ordinary ways were obstructed by rivers or defences of the enemy or felled frees, the soldiers had to retreat with the greatest difficulty through forests and mountain passes and defiles, over flooded fields and on slippery soil, all the while engage the enemy, without food for fifteen days at a stretch." [2]

The Fathers in the mission-stations were recalled by the Superior on the first news of the revolt, and managed to make their way safe to Colombo, "with great difficulty" and "to the great danger of their lives" not only from the enemy but also from fire and sword. The temporary churches were all burned down by the rebels except the one at a place "three leagues from Colombo" which is probably Weligampitiya.

All the Fathers were assembled in Colombo in the Lent of 1603 and their number was far more than could be usefully employed in the city. Fathers Pedro Euticio and Sebastian Andrelli were therefore sent back to India, the former to continue his studies, the latter to

[1] Diego da Cunha, 10 December 1603.
[2] Alberto Laertio, S.J., 13 January 1604.

labour on the Fishery Coast. The others began preacning Lenten sermons, hearing confessions, giving instructions in religious knowledge in public and private, till, as one expressed it, "the people of Colombo, who were formerly ill instructed in the faith are now thoroughly versed therein and are no longer wild trees of vice but bring forth the cinnamon and balsamum of virtue." [1]

Azevedo had intended to found a Jesuit College in Colombo "but as he has sustained much loss in this revolt and has spent what he had in this Island, he is not able to carry out his intention now." When at last he succeeded in reducing the country to obedience he granted on 22 October 1603, the revenues of the villages of Munessaram, Moratuwa and Kohilawatte. In February 1604, he also gave the College for a villa house a land "encircled by a small lake, to make an orchard of it for the recreation of the Fathers of the College, although part of it was already planted with palm trees; but at present more is spent on it then it yields." [2]

This endowment was intended to maintain the Fathers engaged in College work. The villages, however, at first yielded nothing, and Azevedo in his liberality gave "each year 600 *zerafins*." [3] The Fathers living in the missions received each 10 *zerafins* from the royal treasury for their upkeep. One of the Fathers of the College took charge of Moratuwa, were some seventy persons, who had so far not become Christians, were duly instructed and baptized. "Nowhere in Ceylon are there such fervent Catholics as at Moratuwa," [4] which was completely a Christian village, not more than six or seven of the inhabitants being non-Christians.

[1] Pedro Euticio, S.J., 15 October 1605.
[2] Ms. Foundation and Origin of the College of Colombo.
[3] The silver equivalent of the *pardao*.
[4] Pedro Euticio, S.J., 15 October 1605.

CHAPTER VIII

The Mission Stations

AS soon as the subjugation of the revolted districts permitted it, work was resumed in the mission stations. Kammala and Chilaw had given such promise of being fruitful fields for evangelization that the Provincial of Malabar, Father Alberto Laertio, who had come to make a visitation of the Jesuit mission in Ceylon, would not return to India till he had re-established the mission stations. He therefore set out in 1604 accompanied by Fathers Balthazar Garcia and Lambert Ruiz, and labouriously rebuilt the churches and formally opened the mission. These two missionaries were especially chosen for the task on account of their great experience in India, their mildness and charity, and above all for their thorough knowledge of the Tamil language.

CHILAW

The result of their labours fully justified the expectations, for in a very short time the people of Chilaw were duly instructed. The missionary then decided to celebrate the baptism of the chief men with solemnity. The five Pattankattis, when fully grounded in the faith, were taken to Malwana for the feast of Our Lady of Victories as that was the day on which the whole island assembled to pay customary homage to the Captain-General who represented the King of Portugal. In Sinhalese courts this ceremony used to be called the *perahera*, and consisted in a muster of the states and payment of tribute. On this solemn occasion the five Pattankattis were baptized with great ceremony in the presence of the Portuguese officials and the Sinhalese chiefs. The new converts returned to Chilaw laden with honours and favours. The rest of the people were baptized in Chilaw itself. Four years later when the Bishop of Cochin paid his diocesan visit he confirmed the converts.

The Jesuit Church of Chilaw was built in the heart of the inhabited quarter of the village, and as the people were within easy reach of the pastor, he was able to give his whole attention to their formation in the practice of the Catholic faith. Such solicitude was the more necessary in the case of adult converts whose perseverance depended in no small measure on the solidity of the instruction and the regularity of the practice of the faith. Accordingly only those who showed special aptitude for this laborious work were put in charge of important mission centres. In Chilaw catechism lessons were given twice a day to the young; in the morning to the girls and in the evening to the boys. Schools were also set up in each station for the secular education of the children. This work was so effectively done in Chilaw that the missionary records with pride that his flock consisted of Catholics 'as well instructed and devout as one could possibly wish for.' Even those who did not embrace Christianity in the beginning are said to have conceived so high an esteem for the truth and purity of the Christian religion that few dared to face death unbaptized. A dramatic performance is given every year on the feast of the Church to the delight and edification of all. [1]

[1] Pero Francisco, 2 December, 1612.

The duty of ministering to so large a flock was found to be too much for Father Ruiz, and in 1609 Father Emmanuel Campellus, who had previously worked in Mannar, was sent to help him. But the veteran missionary continued to work so assiduously that he wore himself out and fell dangerously ill. He was immediately removed to Colombo where he died on the very day of his arrival, 28th December 1611, in the 62nd year of his age and 21st of missionary activity in the East. He was by birth a Dutchman, and was one of those early Jesuits who had made the language of the country so particularly his own that he scarcely ever used any other. He was often employed by his superiors to teach Tamil to the other missionaries which he did with great care and accuracy. He was born at Colombeo in Gelderen and entered the Society at the age of 30, having been sometime in the service of Cardinal Perugini. He came to India when still a novice and laboured chiefly in Travancore, nine years at Periapatanam and some years as Superior of Negapatam, and came to Ceylon in 1604. He died praying in Tamil, and his place was taken by Father Mathew Fernandez.

The Church of Chilaw continued to flourish with wonderful rapidity and the annual letters record the progress made year after year.[1] In 1613 there was received into the Church an *Arache* who is declared to be 'the foremost man of those parts in birth.' In the following year two hundred adults were baptized includ-

[1] The success of the Jesuits in the Seven Korales stirred the Franciscans, and Father Francis Negrao, the Commissary, went in 1610 on an apostolic tour in their district with Friar Antonio de San Thome who knew Sinhalese, and held 31 general baptisms in five months at Nawagamuwa, Kelaniya, Halpe, Panadura, Kalutara, Maggona, Alutgama, Galle, Mipe, Weligama, Matara, Madampe and Welitota; after which he went to Rome to report on it to the Pope and the Cardinals. *Conquista Spiritual do Oriente* Ms. Ch.-33.

ing " the old women of the ten chief families " who had held out long, unwilling to break away from lifelong associations of worship. The increase of the flock necessitated a larger church and a new one was built on another site.

To the church of Chilaw were attached Madampe and Munnessaram and from 1609 two priests were stationed in the Residence.[1] The former served a flock scattered over twelve villages situated far from each other. Converts were added every year and the annual letters tell of one, a young man, the son of an influential Brahmin, who came to baptism in state, mounted on an elephant and attended by a train of soliders and by his kith and kin who were not Christians. In 1614 the number of converts made amounted to 800. In the church of Madampe was buried Father Gaspar de Abreu, one of the most successful missionaries of the time, who died there on his way from Kalpitiya to Colombo on 22 December 1614. Born at Valenca do Minho in 1548, he entered the Society in 1578 and worked on the Fishery Coast since 1585. In 1603 he was captured by the Vadagars at Tuticorin but was ransomed by the Christians 18 days later for 4,000 *cruzados*. When the Jesuits were expelled from the coast, he was so inconsolable that the Superiors sent him to Ceylon and stationed him at Kalpitiya where he converted the whole island.

The church of Munnessaram, dedicated to the Apostle St. Paul was built on the site of the pagan temple destroyed by the Portuguese. Fourteen of the principal men of the place embraced Christianity at the very outset and even those who had formerly been in the service of the temple became Christians. The inhabitants

[1] Christopher Joam, 1 December, 1609.

of Palanchena, which is close to Munnessaram, all promised to become Christians as soon as the church was built.

KAMMALA

The mission of Kammala was begun at the same time as Chilaw by Father Balthazar Garcia. Here too, as in Chilaw, the people all embraced Christianity in a body, and their number is said to have been greater than at Chilaw. In 1608 an epidemic broke out in the village and the pastor was so assiduous in looking after his flock that not one of the seventy Christians who fell victims to the disease met his death without being fortified by the Christian sacraments. The Father himself caught the contagion and was removed to Colombo, another priest taking his place. The new converts were not only fully instructed in the principles and practice of the Christian faith and morals but were successfully weaned of the many superstitious habits intervowen into their social and domestic life and hallowed by lifelong observance. A flourishing Tamil school was set up for the secular education of the young whose intelligence and marvellous powers of memory evoked the admiration of the Archbishop of Goa who happened to visit the place.

One of the Christian devotions introduced by the missionaries and destined to become very popular with the converts of these parts was the devotion to the Holy Cross. That symbol of Christianity was planted before every church and presbytery : crosses were worn round the necks and carried in procession ; and crosses were in great demand for the sick and the dying. In times of drought intercessory processions were organized in honour of the Cross and on almost all occasions downpours of rain are said to have fallen in answer to prayer. The people of the place are described as " extremely kind and gentle" and were so well-disposed to the new religion that great hopes were entertained of converting the whole country. As the church was found to be too small for the increasing congregation, a more commodious church was built on another site and was adorned with an excellent picture of the adoration of the infant Jesus by the Magi, placed above the main altar. On the feast of the Church there was always a dramatic representation which gives "great pleasure to the people and is much admired by the gentiles."

In 1616—17 the tumults of war greatly impeded the work of evangelization. "These wars are indeed a great obstacle to the spread of the faith" declared a missionary. And so in fact it proved, for most of the churches in this part of the island were destroyed by the rebels in the course of the warfare that began in 1616.

KALPITIYA

The peninsula of Kalpitiya "lying between Chilaw and Puttalam" and "separated from the mainland by a narrow estuary" was given to the College of Cochin as its endowment.[1] It was a desolate and sterile tract of waste, very sparsely populated. The people received the missionary with great benevolence "not because they liked the Portuguse, but because they knew that they would be safe under the protection of the Fathers." In 1610 there were two Fathers in charge of the three churches of Kalpitiya, one maintained by the College of Cochin, the other by the state.[2] They had to labour with great difficulty for not only was the country sterile and the climate severe but there were repeated droughts

[1] *Documentos Remettidos da India* I 247.
[2] Foundation and Origin.

and the people had not the wherewith to support life. The continuous heat of the three successive years 1608-1610 compelled the people to seek a sustenance in another part of the island.

One of the missionaries brought a colony of Christians from India to cultivate the lands. They cleared the woods and set an example to the very backward inhabitants of Kalpitiya. They received weekly instruction, for they were away in the forests for five days at a stretch and returned to their habitations on Saturday to receive instruction in preparation for the Lord's day. Eventually Father Gaspar de Abreu converted all the inhabitants of Kalpitiya except the Moors. The first three churches of this mission were at Kalpitiya, Maripo and Nallacalli.

MALWANA

Though Malwana was not a mission-station, the priest who lived with the Captain-General had many opportunities of preaching the gospel on account of the constant contact with the Sinhalese people which his position in the General's camp gave him. For this reason the Superior of the mission sent thither those who wished to gain proficiency in the Sinhalese language. The Father at Malwana often carried on controversy with the gentiles and when their difficulties were solved and questions answered they, not unfrequently, asked for baptism. The Father, however, did not baptize them himself, but when he had converted and instructed them, he despatched them to the Franciscans or to Colombo for baptism. It was in this way that one of the most prominent converts of the time, Alagiyawanna Mukaveti, the great Sinhalese poet, was directed to the Jesuit College of Colombo for enlightenment in the Christian religion. He went to the Jesuit College and told the

Fathers that he desired to be instructed in the Christian faith and inquired what Jesus Christ had done and left in writing. Being told of the Christian gospels the poet set himself to read the New Testament "with so much attention and ardour that in less than six months there was not a passage which he could not recite, for he had acquired Latin very thoroughly. After having been well-instructed he told the Fathers that he wished to receive holy baptism, as he saw that their religion was the good and true one and such as Jesus Christ had taught. But what astonished him was that they did not follow Christ's example, because according to the gospels, He never took money from anyone, while they on the contrary took it from everyone and neither baptized nor buried anyone without it. This did not prevent him from being baptized and from working for the conversion of others afterwards."[1] "The children are taught letters in the School and the Christian doctrine is imparted in church," to Sinhalese "in their mother tongue" to others "in Portuguese"[2]

The Father stationed at Malwana was also able to convert several young princes. Mention is made in the Jesuit writings of three sons of a prince of Uva, and the son of a chieftain unnamed. These young men were sent to the Jesuit College of Colombo where they were educated with the sons of the Portuguese.

The Father of Malwana was also able to render a great service to the Church by providing Catholic writings in the vernacular. In 1610 he is said to have been

[1] *Travels in India* by Jean Baptiste Tavernier. Volume II, Book III, Chapter 4. Ball's translation II, 148. About Alagiyawanna, see his Christian poem, *Kustantinu Hatana*, critically edited by Father S. G. Perera, S.J., and Mr. M. E. Fernando; Colombo, Catholic Press, 1932.

[2] Francisco Cagnola, 9 December, 1610.

"almost entirely occupied in perfecting his knowledge of Sinhalese, which can be better done here than anywhere else. He has already translated into that language some Prayers, a Catechism, the principal events of Our Lord's Life and some anecdotes of the Saints."[1] In this work he is said to have made use of the help of an old pundit who afterwards became a Catholic and took in baptism the name of his god-father, Siman Correa, and helped "to translate 26 Lives of Saints, and compose an Explanation of the Seven Sacraments and other Sinhalese works."[2]

MATIYAGAMA

The most important mission-centre in the purely Sinhalese part of the country was at Matiyagama or Metiyagama[3] in the Seven Korales. This mission was begun in 1610 at the instance of Siman Correa who was at the time Disawa of the Seven Korales and had invited a Jesuit Father to his capital. He wished to establish a settlement at Maityagama "with which to attack the enemy's territory and come to our assistance when we are attacked." Before the Father arrived, Correa himself "exhorted the people of Matiyagama and the leading men of the Seven Korales to embrace the Christian faith, saying that it was time to think of the salvation of one's soul; that the worship of idols was a vain superstition; that Christ alone was God, whom all men must serve to save their souls."[4]

When he had thus prepared the ground the Father arrived and worked so diligently that in six months about 600 people placed themselves under instruction and

[1] Francisco Cagnola, 9 December, 1610.
[2] Pero Francisco, 2 December, 1612. Cf. Appendix No. 10.
[3] The old name is Matiyagama.
[4] Christopher Joam, December, 1611.

were baptized. Three hundred others were being prepared for baptism when the Father took ill and had to interrupt the work. The Jesuits had introduced to Ceylon the use of quinine or the "Jesuit Bark" for fever, and we may well suppose that they themselves used what they often gave to others. On his return he began the work of building a church, but the absence of Correa and his men who had gone to Uva and Batticaloa and the ill-health of the Father greatly delayed the work. Another Father was sent to assist the missionary. Siman Correa bore the cost of the church and gave a palm grove for the support of the missionary.

Finally on 13 January 1611 the church of Matiyagama was blessed by the Rector of the Jesuit College of Colombo who sang the first Mass therein and administered baptism to 150 new converts. These were "principal captains and native soliders. There was besides a Bandara, that is to say a Prince, three Mudaliyars many Araches and distinguished lascarins" and the "son of an Adigar." This last "who was named Lawrence died soon afterwards and his father wanted to cremate him, as is their custom. But the missionary objected and with the school children, who sang the prayers in Sinhalese, took the body to the church where it was buried, and the people who had never seen this mode of burial were quite pleased."[1] Among the 280 persons baptized in 1615 were "six persons of royal blood, many Mudaliyars and Araches, and a Captain of the King of Kandy." Others were baptized later, bringing the total for that year to 400. The number of Bandaras increased to six and many people, nay "thousands, are ready to embrace Christianity."[2]

[1] Pero Francisco, 2 December, 1612.

[2] Ib.

MAKANDURA

The success of Matiyagama soon led to the establishment of another mission station in the Seven Korales, called Makandura at a "distance of two leagues from Matiyagama." Nearly all the people of the village placed themselves under instruction, and the Father built them a church. Makandura is now at the 10th mile post on the road to the Chilaw district from Giriulla. About half a mile on the Giriulla side of the Rest House, south of the high road, is *Palliye-godelle-watta*,[1] now a field. The high land close by is *Palliye-godelle-wala-watte*, which is probably the site of the old church.[2]

The current use of the Sinhalese language made these two Fathers of Matiyagama and Makandura greatly popular. "The confidence with which the gentiles, not only of the conquered territories, but even of the enemy's kingdom, treat the Fathers is really remarkable. When the subjects of the King of Kandy come down to our province, the first thing they do is to visit the Fathers. Even the King of Kandy when he has some business with the Portuguese, as he had on four occasions, sends his ambassadors to the Fathers with *olas*,[3] and it is only to the Fathers that he sends *olas*."[4] The Disawa of the Seven Korales attributed this influence of the Fathers to the fact they "had gained the hearts of the Sinhalese by their sincerity, goodness and kindness."

In fact when small-pox broke out in the Seven Korales and the victims were abandoned by their kith

[1] Sinhalese for "the garden of the highland of the (Christian) Church".

[2] Information kindly conveyed to me from Makandura during a circuit, by Mr. H. W. Codrington then Govt. Agent of the North Western Province, on 21—9—26.

[3] Letters written on palm-leaves.

[4] Em. Barradas, 24 November, 1613.

and kin, it was the Fathers alone who visited the afflicted. And a Budhist monk who watched the Father paying his usual rounds, was so much struck by the kindness of the Father towards the suffering, towards whom he himself felt an aversion, that moved by the grace of God he placed himself under instruction to became a Christian.[1]

MORATUWA

Moratuwa being close to Colombo the Father in charge lived in the College, except for special reasons as when a contagion broke out there. The Father then remained at Moratuwa "to be at hand to administer the sacraments." He procured medicine for the sick from Colombo. "Almost all the people of Moratuwa are Christians, and as they live close to us, they are well-instructed also. If any stranger comes to the village the people exhort him to become a Christian."[2]

[1] Em. Barradas l. c.
[2] Christopher Joam, 1 December, 1609.

CHAPTER IX

The Destruction of the Mission and the Martyrdom of two Missionaries

THE success of the missions in the Sinhalese territory provoked the anger "of the enemy of mankind," who thereupon "stirred up hostilities between the Portuguese and the Sinhalese." Such was the comment of a Jesuit on the tumultuous warfare that broke out in 1616, and caused the death of the two missionaries of Matiyagama and Makandura and the destruction of churches. It was so unexpected and disastrous an event that we have several accounts of the occurrence sent to Rome and Lisbon. The story is thus narrated by Father Manoel Barradas.

"The Missionary of Makandura, Joao Metalla, a Portuguese who had built a church there with great labour thought of baptizing his converts with more than usual solemnity, and set out for Colombo to procure the necessary ornaments. On his way thither, he paid a visit to Father Luis Mattheus Pelingotti at Matiyagama. These two Fathers, who were working together for the salvation of souls, were not only great friends, but also so alike in their zeal and natural dispositions, that they were greatly beloved by the people of the country, both for their kindness and because of their great familiarity with the Sinhalese language. But the Divine Husbandman, wishing to gather from the garden of Ceylon two flowers, or rather fruits—for flowers they were, if we consider their age and fulness of hope, but ripe fruits if we look at the gravity of their life and suavity of manners—arranged matters in the following way, when they were together at Matiyagama.

On Tuesday the sixth of December, 1616, there came to Matiyagama, fifty of the Ceylonese soldiers called lascarins, from the city of Kandy. They did not hide their hostile intentions, and the inhabitants were somewhat alarmed by their unexpected appearance. Four of these soldiers made their way to the house of the Fathers, and by their kind words persuaded the servants at the door to call Father Pelingotti, pretending that they had some good news to tell the Father and were bearers of a letter for him from Captain Francis de Silva. This captain had been appointed by the General of the Island, Nuno Alvares Pereira, to take the place of Philip de Oliveira, Disawa of the Seven Korales, who was giving chase to the rebel Barreto.[1]

Father Pelingotti thereupon came out with Father Metella to hear, as they thought, the news of some victory. The Father soon perceived that the pretended messenger was a cheat, for as soon as the Father asked him about the victory, he replied that his companions who were coming would describe it in detail. These companions came up immediately, fully armed, and began to cause an uproar, and forming bands, guarded every possible way of escape. The rest crowded round the Fathers on all sides, thirsting for their blood. Father Pelingotti taken by surprise, asked the spokesman, what was the meaning of this armed crowd.

[1] Antonio Barreto, a renegade Christian lascarin, who was in revolt, 1603—1620, and became master of the two disawas of Matara and Sabaragamuwa ("Kuruviti Rala") and finally King of Uva. He was slain in 1620. About his career, see *Kustantinu Hatana*.

Thereupon the messenger gave the signal and the massacre began. A spear flung at Father Pelingotti ran him through the abdomen. As he fell he made a sign to his companion, Father Metella, to escape, and raised his eyes to heaven in prayer. Then dragging himself to the foot of a cross, he grasped it as best he could, and gave up his happy soul to his Creator. Thus this ardent missionary received the reward for his virtue, which he had always desired, for I heard from Father Nicholas Levanto that it was Father Pelingotti's constant prayer to lay down his life for God. Father Luis Mattheus Pelingotti was an Italian born at Sorbolongi in the diocese of Fossombrone in the States of the Church. After his priesthood he became tutor to the children of a noble family of Rome and was on the point of entering a brilliant career, when he made an act of self-renunciation and decided to become a Jesuit. Two years later he set out for the Missions and was sent to Ceylon. He died full of merits, in the 39th year of his age, having spent 14 years in the Society. *Consummatus in brevi explevit tempora multa.*

"Meanwhile Father Metella tried to make his way to the house of Philip de Oliveira, but was overtaken by two lascarins who transpierced his body with lances. Raising his eyes to heaven and extending his hands in prayer, he boldly faced his murderers ready to receive further wounds from which he fell dead. Father Joao Metalla was born in the town of Bomjardin and set out for India in 1603 at the age of 18, and at the time of his death he was 32 years old, of which 17 were spent in the Society.

"These two Fathers confessed the name of Christ unto blood, and the barbarous people, in carrying out the designs of heaven, put their bodies together at the foot of the cross, so that those who were so united in life might not be separated in death. Their heads were cut off and fixed on spears, of which one was planted before the older temple and the other before the new. Such was the happy end of the two Fathers who in order to spread the Christian faith gave up their lives to the Redeemer, rendering blood for blood.

A young man, a servant of the Fathers, was an eye-witness to this spectacle so agreeable to God and his angels. His life too was threatened by the wicked men, who gave him chase, but as he left them the keys of the house and of the church, they delayed long enough for him to make his escape, for fear added wings to his feet. With these keys the soldiers entered the church and the presbytery and destroyed everything, committing barbarous turpitudes which showed them to be declared enemies of the faith; for they took hold of a crucifix that was in the room of Father Pelingotti, and bringing it out, they broke the cross, wrested the image from it, broke its arms and legs, cut off the nose and mouth, shamefully disfigured the right cheek, and threw the truncated image, which they had so irreverently treated, on the dead bodies of the Fathers.

The dead bodies were afterwards found, and the Crucifix is still preserved. This murder, so glorious to us and so baneful to the enemy, was the beginning of disturbances. The esteem in which the Fathers were held was so great that their relics were diligently sought for. Many people carry about them handkerchiefs stained in their blood: others treasure their fingernails or hair. Portions of their garments and the mutilated crucifix are preserved with great honour in the College."

Many reasons are assigned for this murder, but the most likely one seems to be this. "There were many other Portuguese whom it would have been easier to attack, many towns better suited for the overthrow of the Portuguese. But they chose to lay hands on the Fathers, so that frightened by the atrocity of the deed, the supporters of the rebellion might never put themselves in the power of the Portuguese or trust their treaties or think they could live safe under Portuguese laws." This seems to be the most satisfactory explanation because the rebellion, though not due to religious hatred, began with an attack on priests and churches, merely to make the rebels burn their boats.

"For a full understanding of this rebellion[1] it is good to give an account of the leader who plotted and contrived it. This was a man called Nikapitiya, a native of Rayigam Korale, son of a *pattinihamy* which means a religious woman that served in their temples, by a *Maninna*, which means 'measurer.' His birth place was Medagama in Rayigam Korale and he had some connection with Welikala Ralahamy, a man of princely birth. This Nikapitiya grew up from his boyhood and had some dealings with the Portuguese as he was a servant of a Franciscan friar named Friar Manoel da Trinidade, the first Rector of Kalutara. When he was a grown up lad he married the daughter of Pulosinga Arache of Waddu-Potupitiya. Then he went to Malwana in 1606 and took service under Domingos da Costa the overseer of the General Don Jeronimo de Azevedo. When Azevedo became Viceroy this Nikapitiya became the *vidana* in charge of the villages of a Captain named Simao de Lemos, a gallant man who fell in warfare at Kandy. He then became the *vidana* of the palankeen bearers of the Captain-General, Francisco de Menezes; and when Don Francisco left he continued to serve the Captain-General Manoel Mascarenhas in the same capacity. At this time

[1] Antonio Bocarro *Decada XIII* pp. 496—8.

he crept into the favour of a queen of Walgama from whom he learnt a good many stories of the relationship between the kings of the island. Moreover he was at this time not living with the wife whom he married, for which and for many other complaints, for he was a saucy fellow, the Fathers urged him to live with his wife; and on one occasion he even received a good thrashing, when coming from Kandy he fell in with a number of elephants that Antonio Batalha was taking to Jaffna for Manoel Mascarenhas Homem, just a year before this rebellion.

When Nikapitiya reached Jaffna in that company it would seem that some evil spirit entered into him, for he planned the trick which he carried out within a few days, giving out that he was the Sinhalese prince that went to Portugal and died at Coimbra,[1] as he bore the name of Nikapitiya. He thus let his hair grow, and clothed himself in skins like a *yogi* and made his way to Anuradhapura, and there he made himself known to a headman of the Seven Korales, named Kalugampola Rala who had escaped from Siman Correa. He claimed to be the Prince above mentioned and expressed great sorrow for the state of his kingdom which he had come from Portugal at great trouble and risk to restore to its former liberty. In this way he got in touch with the people of the Seven Korales where the return of the Prince was noised about among all some months before he showed himself in public.

At this time Don Nuno Alvares Pereira was General and Philip de Oliveira was Disawa of the Seven Korales whom the General sent with the Disawa of Matara to

[1] Nikapitiya Bandara, grandson of Raja Sinha, who became a Christian under the name of Don Philip, was educated at Goa, where he received Minor Orders, and went thence to the University of Coimbra in Portugal where he died.

make war on the Two Korales bordering on Uva. Profiting by this absence the rebel who was in the neighbourhood entered Matiyagama on the fifth of December 1616 as king, and killed the Fathers of the Society, making the people of Matiyagama themselves take part in the deed so that becoming guilty of murder before us they might follow him. Thus giving out that he was the King with the name which they had heard previously to be his, he declared that he had come to free them from subjection to us and make them the lords of the country; and the revolt spread so rapidly that in less than eight days he received the allegiance of the whole country and the King of Kandy sent him two thousand men under the command of Kangara Arache and Kuruppu Mudaliyar."

CHAPTER X

Resumption of Mission Work

THE rebellion of the pretender Nikapitiya was a severe blow to the mission. Churches were destroyed, mission houses levelled to the ground, and the Christians who remained faithful to their religion, exposed to most bitter trials. They often found themselves between two fires. The rebels treated them as supporters of the Portuguese, while the latter in their turn often visited them with the punishment reserved for treachery. The missionaries were not on the spot to protect them from the Portuguese, for the Rector of the College fearing for their lives summoned them all to Colombo. Even Moratuwa, which was unaffected by the revolt, was found insecure, and the missionary who had recently built a new church and presbytery there was ordered to betake himself to the College, whence he managed to visit his flock at intervals. Fifteen Fathers were thus assembled in the College of Colombo, who having nothing else to do gave themselves fervently to spiritual exercises and lachrymation. The presence of these refugees brought the Rector face to face with an embarrassing problem of domestic economy, for the resources of the College straitened by the revolt, were quite unequal to the task of supporting so numerous a household. On such occasions the Rector generally sent some to India. This time, however, a timely donation from the townspeople saved the missionaries.

Fortunately for the Portuguese, Nikapitiya soon fell out with the King of Kandy who thereupon sought to join hands with the Portuguese against him. On 15 March, 1617, the King sent two prisoners-of-war to Malwana to broach the question of peace. They also brought a letter from the King to the Jesuit Superior asking for his intervention in the matter. The Gėneral, Nuno Alvares Pereira, was willing to make terms, and as a result of this preliminary move a formal embassy from Kandy arrived at Malwana on 6th May and was conducted to Colombo where the General summoned a Council in which Father Manoel Rodriguez, the Rector of the College took part. The peace was finally signed by both parties[1] in August, 1617, and the missionaries were able to return to their posts.

They found their work undone. It was not merely the "material edifices" that were destroyed, says one, but what was more painful to them, the "spiritual edifice" of souls. The converts were discouraged, scattered, and had been without any instruction or sacrament or act of Catholic worship for months. There was no help for it but to begin the work anew. The church and the mission house of Moratuwa were still standing and the missionary was enabled to take up his abode there. At Kammala the church was repaired. The church of Chilaw was transferred to another site whither the Christians migrated. The mission of Munnessaram was not resumed for a time. In the Kalpitiya peninsula the missionary stationed himself at Tatai[2] to look after the four churches, for all the inhabitants, except some Moors, had embraced the Christian religion. Very soon even

[1] See "The First Treaty of Peace between the Portuguese and the King of Kandy, 1617" by Father S. G. Perera, S.J., *Ceylon Literary Register* II and III.

[2] Tataya also called Tatavila.

the Moors were brought into the fold and two thousand persons were baptized at Navalcare.[1] The perilous stations of Matiyagama and Makandura were not resumed for a time, but only visited at intervals by a missionary or by the military chaplain. The priest stationed at Malwana was so eager to return to his post that not even the floods of the Kelaniya could prevent him.

The Christians who had suffered at the hands of the rebels or of the Portuguese troops were soon relieved by the missionary. To purchase the liberty of those sold to slavery was easy enough, but the trouble they had to obtain the pardon of those condemned to death, is described as " by no means contemptible." However, no effort was spared and the influence of the Fathers finally carried the day. An order was obtained that, " no Christian be put to death." The prisoners were accordingly led forth to be discharged and many a Buddhist, eager to profit by the windfall, piously made the sign of the cross on his forehead and passed for a Christian. The missionaries who were ready to make the most of any circumstance found great satisfaction in this imposture, for one naively remarks, "It will at least make them embrace the Christian faith more readily in the future."

For a time the missionaries laid aside all attempts at conversion and occupied themselves solely with the converts already made, for though the King of Kandy made peace with the Portuguese, the fire of rebellion had burst out even against the Kandyan monarch for coming to terms with the Portuguese. Two powerful rebels against the Portuguese were at large, Antonio Barreto and Kangara Arache.[2] These two also joined hands, attacked the

[1] Nawatkadn.

[2] A native of Alutkuru Korale, in revolt 1603—1620.

King of Kandy, and sent a message to Mayadunna,[1] a Sinhalese Prince of Uva who had fled to South India, to come and place himself at the head of another rebellion against the Portuguese as well as against the Sinhalese monarch. The missionaries were therefore in constant dread that warfare would soon be resumed. The arrival of Constantine de Sa as General of Ceylon, however, changed the face of affairs. De Sa gave battle to the united forces as described by the Christian poet Alagiyawanna in his *Kustantinu Hatana,* or the 'Campaign of Constantine.' After their rout at Lellopitiya, Kangara Arache was beheaded, Mayadunna fled to Trincomalie where he attempted to entreat, without success, the support of the Danes who had come to Ceylon under Ove Giedde to fish in troubled waters. Mayadunna was finally obliged to return to India, and Baretto was slain. It was only after this military success that the missionaries were enabled to work in peace. The messenger who had gone to India to summon Mayadunna was a Christian of Kalpitiya. But when he realized, "that the Portuguese were always victorious he returned to Kalpitiya, where he had denied his faith. But falling grieviously ill he sought the hospitality of Munnessaram. The Father hearing that he was ill paid him a visit. Being asked why he came thither, the man, knowing that he was in danger of death, replied that he had returned to give himself over to the Portuguese General and undergo the death he had deserved. His end, however, was near, and he soon came to such good dispositions as to make a general confession of the sins of his whole life past, shedding tears of repentance. In a few days he lost consciousness and breathed his last, to the great solace of all who had reason to think

[1] A descendant of Mayadunna of Sitawake and cousin of Dona Catherina.

that he went to the place which is open to those who die well."[1]

The success of Constantine de Sa led to great activity on the part of the missionaries. The Jesuits were invited to open a College in Galle and to evangelize the newly reduced province of Jaffna. The success of the Jaffna mission was so great that it eclipsed all others, and a description of that mission will be given in a later chapter. Meanwhile the Jesuit College of Colombo was severely tried by a calamity which threatened to destroy it altogether. The College had been founded by Azevedo who endowed it with the revenues of some royal villages gifted by Don Joao Periapandar, the last King of Kotte, to the Franciscans for educational purposes. As the donor's wish had not been carried out at the time, the civil and ecclesiastical authorities concurred in conveying these lands to the Jesuits for the same purpose. In time of peace the villages yielded an income sufficient to support the Fathers engaged in College work or being prepared for the mission. Moreover the lands, especially the Kalpitiya peninsula, had been cleared and cultivated by the Jesuits with great trouble. The revolts reduced the revenues, but soon after the rebellion of Nikapitiya even the legality of the gift was disputed and the endowment summarily withdrawn.

The reason for this hasty step was the following. It would seem that when the affairs of Ceylon held out prospects of an increase of the dominion of the Portuguese, the Duke of Villahermosa called upon the Viceroy of India to exert himself for the promotion of education in Ceylon, pointing out that the grants of the Christian King of Kotte were made for that express purpose. A Cont-

[1] Emmanuel de Costa 15 December 1618.

roller of Revenue sent by the King of Portugal had been busy for some time compiling a ponderous Tombo or register of the royal revenues in Ceylon. The Viceroy who was hostile to the Jesuits, therefore, opined that the best means to carry out the royal mandate was to withdraw the endowment from the College and transfer the lands to the Franciscans. Therefore in concert with the new Bishop of Cochin, who was also not very friendly towards the Jesuits, the lands were withdrawn. The Franciscans were at the same time invited to use the revenues to establish schools in Colombo, Galle, and Negombo, as they proposed to do.

The Jesuits were in consternation. The Rector of Colombo, an Italian named Antonio Rubino, who at the request of the Captain-General had even used his influence with the Nayaka of Madura to avert a union between that ruler and the Danes, made every effort to save the College and represented matters to the authorities in Lisbon and Goa. Finally after a couple of years the new Governor of India restored the endowment for three years pending a final decision of the King of Portugal. This decision came in due course and the College was saved. While these negotiations were proceeding the College had to shift as best it could. The townspeople of Colombo stood by the Jesuits and subscribed generously for their maintenance. The death at this juncture of Mercia Roiz, the rich widow who had bequeathed her property to the College subject to a life allowance for herself, enabled the Fathers to tide over that difficulty.

Upon the restoration of the lands, churches were erected at Weligampitiya, Udugampola, Mabodale, and Kohilawatta, which were villages belonging to the College, and also in the forts of Batticaloa and Trincomalie which were in the mission field allotted to the

Society. They also completed the new Jesuit Church of Colombo, and began to rebuild the College on an enlarged plan.

In the College there died in 1626 the Ceylonese Jesuit, Emmanuel de Costa, who was the first to compile a Grammar of the Sinhalese language in a foreign tongue. He was a Portuguese born in Colombo and educated in that very College. After his preparatory studies he was ordained priest in 1620. "Of him," writes Joam Carvalho, "we were deprived by a premature death in the prime of his life, to the great grief and loss not only of ours but even of the whole city; for he was indeed a man not only remarkable for piety but also accomplished in every line, an eminent preacher, so well versed in the language that he composed an excellent Sinhalese Grammar and translated many works well calculated to fortify the Catholics in their faith and to make the gentiles detest their errors.........All the hopes we entertained about him were shattered by his death. His funeral was as well attended as it could possibly be in this city, and the people, the clergy and the regulars, vied with each other in showing their esteem of him. He died on 15th July (1626) in the 36th year of his age, 18th in the Society."

CHAPTER XI

The Development of the Mission

IT was during the period of administration of Don Constantine de Sa de Noronha that the Jesuit Missions in Ceylon attained their fullest development. De Sa was a man of great integrity and valour, a good Christian and an able administrator. He was twice general of Ceylon, first from 1618 to 1619 when he crushed the rebellion, and again from 1623 to 1630 when he extended the sway of Portugal and came by his death on the field of battle. According to a report signed by him in 1628[1] the Franciscan friars had 54 churches with 17,074 Christians in the kingdom of Kotte alone. About the same time the Jesuit churches, though less numerous, were spread about in the Seven Korales, in the villages granted to the College of Colombo, in Mannar and in the kingdom of Jaffna. All the churches in the South were under the direction of the Rector of the College of Colombo, who was Superior Regular of the missionaries. They were grouped under what were called "Residences" of which the number varied and in each of which there was at least one missionary, sometimes two, who visited the churches regularly. The Residence of Galle was of a special kind, being not a mission station, but a religious house with a school, intended to develop into a College.

In 1627 there were ten Residences; in 1628 thirteen. These were Moratuwa, (Malwana), Weligampitiya, Udu-

[1] Conquista Spiritual do Oriente. Ms. ch. 27. Queyroz *Conquista*, pp. 714-719.

gampola, Mabodale, Matiyagama, Makandura, Kammala, Chilaw, Munessaram, Kalpitiya, Aruvichena (Puttalam) and in the new forts of Batticaloa and Trincomalie. In 1644 there was besides a Residence at Etalai to which the church of Puttalam "in the mainland facing Kalpitiya" was attached.

MORATUWA

Moratuwa was the most Southernly Jesuit church, though that town was not in the mission-field allotted to the Jesuits. It was built because Moratuwa had been given to the College of Colombo as its endowment. It was withdrawn from them in 1617 but restored. The church of Moratuwa dedicated to St. Michael, stood "among cool and dense woods"[1] "along the sea-shore."[2] At first it had no resident priest and was visited from Colombo, a Father going there on the eve of Sundays and feast days when "all the people came to Mass with great devotion." Father Manoel Barradas who accompanied the Provincial, Father Pero Francisco, on a visitation, has left a record of some picturesque details of the customs of the people of Moratuwa. "I saw a wedding," he writes "the ceremonies of which being novel I shall describe. The company consists of all the friends and relations, and to decline is the greatest affront. The wedded pair come walking on white cloths with which the ground is successively carpeted and covered above with others of the same kind, which the nearest relatives hold in their extended hands after the fashion of a canopy, which protects them from the sun. The bride is carried in the arms of the nearest relative, and when this one tires another takes his place. The symbols that they carry are

[1] Manoel Barradas 1612.

[2] Andre Lopes 1644.

white discs and candles lighted in the daytime and certain shells which they keep playing on in place of bagpipes. All these are royal symbols which the former kings conceded to this race of people that being strangers they should inhabit the coasts of Ceilon and none but they or those to whom they give leave, can use them." [1] Moratuwa was a completely Christian town. The Jesuits mentioned as labouring in Moratuwa are Pero Euticio (1606) Sebastino Andrelli (1609—1611) and Antonio Dias.

MALWANA

The Residence of Malwana depended on the goodwill of the Captain-General. The priest stationed there was practically a chaplain, not a missionary, and it was only the Generals who esteemed members of the Society that had Jesuit chaplains. These were especially the two old pupils of the Jesuits, Azevedo and de Sa. Father Euticio is said to have exerted great influence on Azevedo,[2] who was at first a cruel and relentless warrior, but from the time that he had a Jesuit with him, he showed a change of heart. As Malwana was not within the mission-field of the Jesuits no Jesuit church existed there. The first chaplain of Malwana, Father Pedro Euticio was instructed by the Provincial to investigate the antiquities of Ceylon, but his death of fever in 1608 put an end to his researches. His successors were Antonio de Abreu and the two Neapolitans, Petrus Johannes Nocita and Luis Mattheus Pelingotti.

[1] Translation of D. W. Ferguson in the *Ceylon Literary Register* IV (1896).

[2] He became Viceroy of India and in 1617 was taken prisoner to Lisbon but never brought to trial. When he died in the dungeon, 9 March 1625, he was buried at the expense of the Jesuits in the sacristy of the Jesuit Church of St. Roque, now a museum.

WELIGAMPITIYA

The Residence of Weligampitiya in the Alutkuru Korale "two and a half leagues to the East of Colombo" was begun only in 1627. Though a church was previously built there, it had to be given up as the village, though given to the College of Colombo for its endowment, was in the district of the Franciscans. After the restoration of the endowment, a Residence was started with the leave of the Bishop of Cochin. A large number of converts was baptized while a still larger number was awaiting instruction. The church was dedicated to St. Francis Xavier who was then recently canonized. It soon became well known for miracles, "but either owing to the negligence of eyewitness or because of their very abundance, they are buried in oblivion. The multitude even of pagans that flock thither bears witness to the favours granted through the Apostle of the East."[1]

UDUGAMPOLA

"Five leagues to the East of Colombo, in the interior, is the Residence of Udugampola." The church is dedicated to Our Lady, and the Christians who numbered more than a thousand were scattered "over an extent of three leagues more or less." Being an agricultural district, Udugampola was often infested by elephants and it is related how the Christians offer up a few ears of paddy at Our Lady's altar to be preserved from depredations."[2]

When the Hollanders first captured Negombo and threatened Colombo, the Rector of the College summoned all the missionaries in this district to Colombo. But the Neapolitan Didacus de Sigueiros who was at Udugampola

[1] J. Caldeiro, 1654.
[2] Costa, 1648.

could not quit his residence "on account of the floods which had submerged the bridge which could not be crossed" as he himself described in a letter to the General of the Society.[1] He gave himself for lost, but nothing happened. He is described as well versed in both Sinhalese and Tamil. His services were requisitioned in the wars as military chaplain, in which capacity he was especially successful in bringing soldiers to repentance. "In the next world Your Reverence will see what the grace of God has accomplished."

MABODALE

The residence of Mabodale in the Dasiya Pattu of Alutkuru Korale, is first mentioned in 1628 when Father Pedro de Sa[2] was in charge of both Udugampola and Mabodale which were not far from each other. But neither the patron of the church nor any information about the Christians of Mabodale is to be found in any of the available letters.

MATIYAGAMA

Matiyagama in the Katugampola Korale "situated about ten leagues from the coast," "five leagues to the East of Udugampola" was in Portuguese times, "a large town with well laid out streets" and was the "capital of the Seven Korales and the seat of the Disawa." The town lay "between two rivers, one large, (Maha Oya) and the other small (Diyahonda-ela)." Now it is an insignificant hamlet about two miles from Giriulla on the road to Dankotuwa. The patron of the church was Our Lady

[1] Sigueiros 1639. Though an Italian he assumed a Portuguese name and signed his letters, "D. Sigueiros de Abreu."

[2] Born 1593 at Caseais Portugal. He was afterwards, in 1644, Superior of Mannar.

(Assumption). The area under the charge of the missionary resident in Matiyagama "extended over twenty leagues, as far as the frontiers of Kandy." There were 4,000 Christians with five churches, but only two in 1644, though "there is room for thirty if only the country were at peace." Among these villages was Visinave. One of the churches which was for a time the seat of a Resident priest was Makandura.

The last missionary of Matiyagama, Father Antonio Pedrosa, like the first, Luis Mattheus Pelingotti, was exposed to great danger. They were both well versed in Sinhalese. Father Pedrosa often served as military chaplain and was wounded and twice captured, once by the Kandyans and once by the Dutch. He was finally killed and beheaded in 1643 while on his way from Matiyagama to the camp of the Portuguese to hear the confessions of the soldiers.

KAMMALA

From Matiyagama, "following the beach towards the North, at a distance of six leagues from Colombo" is the residence of Kammala, dedicated to the Holy Magi. Attached to it was the church of Diyawela dedicated to Our Lady with 400 Christians, and two other churches. On 25 September, 1613, there appeared at the office of the Portuguese Tombo, in Colombo, the chief pattankatti of Kammala named Siman Correa. Before his baptism he bore the name of Naide Appu.

MADAMPE

Madampe was in Portuguese times, "a very important town, and as it was very productive, of old times it used to have princes." In fact Don Jeronimo Alagiyawanna in his capacity of Mohottala of the Portuguese

Tombo, has recorded under date 5th March, 1614, a short history of Madampe. On the death of Tiruve Bandara of Madampe, son-in-law of Bhuvaneka Bahu and father of Don Joao Periapandar, the last king of Kotte, the town of Madampe was given by Rajasinha of Sitawaka to Timbiripole Adahasin, who held it for some years. On his death Rajasinha himself took possession of the village. On his death in 1592 Pamunnugama Hapuhamy held Madampe, but he was put to death by Domingos Correa. Thereupon the town passed into the hands of the Portuguese by whom it was granted to Lancarotte de Seixas.[1]

Seixas was not at all favourable to the missionaries, for a Jesuit Father who visited Madampe in 1612 has left recorded that in that year the missionary had made more than 500 conversions, but in view of the "dispositions of the people he could have made more conversions if only he had the good will of the lord of the village, not by means of gifts to the converts but only with a good countenance and words. Owing to the selfishness of these officials there are good persons who fear that God will take away from the Portuguese what He has given them to cultivate for Him."

The chief church of Madampe was dedicated to the Assumption of Our Lady. There were two other churches, one at Marawila dedicated to St. Francis Xavier, and the other at Katuneriya dedicated to St. Ambrose. There were 1,800 Christians in 1644.

CHILAW

Half a-league's journey from Madampe "by a canal, like the one that leads from Colombo, the greater part of which is covered by cool groves", lies the Residence of

[1] Portuguese Tombo, III 621.

Chilaw with a church dedicated to St. Peter and a Tamil school for children. The chief men of Chilaw were Christians, the names of some of whom are found in the Tombo, viz., Don Francisco, Sepala Mohottiar, Don Simao, Don Manoel and Don Joao, pattankattis of Chilaw. In the inquiry held on 2 September, 1613, to verify the entries of the Tombo they declared that the ancient *olas* were lost in the course of the revolt of Kangara Arachchy.

To the Residence of Chilaw were attached five other churches, of which the chief one was at Anuvilundana, dedicated to Our Lady.

MUNNESSARAM

'About a mile to the East of Chilaw' is the Residence of Munnessaram, noted for its Hindu Temple. There the Jesuits built a church of St. John the Baptist and a Residence. Attached to this Residence were three churches all dedicated to the Holy Cross, at Kokkuluve, Walhena and Chetur. The chief-men, the kannakkapulle and pattankatti were Christians, the former named Don Jeronimo, the latter Dom Pedro Xembradeina, produced old *olas*.

KALPITIYA

"Going from Chilaw towards the North along the sea-shore there is the island of Calpiti" (Kalpitiya) which the Portuguese called also Cardiva and was renowned in Portuguese annals for the victory which in the river that forms it Andre de Furtado de Mendonca gained over the famous corsair Cutimurca. "The length of this island is twelve Sinhalese leagues which are 24 good Portuguese ones and the breadth half a league; so that it may rather be called a tongue of earth or sand, divided from the mainland by a small river which commences at Chilaw and has its outlet,—being there not only a river but a fine arm of the sea—at Calpiti or Cardiva (now Calpentyn), whence the whole island derives its name."[1]

In Kalpitiya there were two Residences with two Fathers in charge of them. The island was divided into six villages,[2] given to the Society. The first Residence was at Calpentyn then called by the inhabitants Arezari[3] from a tree of great size that stood there. The church was dedicated to the Assumption of Our Lady. There was a Tamil school. Attached to this residence was the church of Tatai, patron SS. Peter and Paul.

ETALE

The second Residence of Kalpitiya was at Etale, patron St. Francis Xavier. Attached to this Residence were a number of churches and Christian villages. The churches were, Nolequilim (Narakkaliya) with a church of the Holy Cross; Navelcaru (Navakkadu) with a church of the Assumption; Maripo (Mampuri ?) with a church of the Holy Cross, and Puttalam "on the mainland in front of Kalpitiya," in which was the church of St. Francis Xavier. Formerly the church of Puttalam was a Residence. It was begun by Father Pedro Euticio in 1602 at Aruvichena, Latinized into Alavichensis, a village now partly within the local Board limits. Father Luis Mattheus Pelingotti had his residence there in 1610–11. But Etale soon came into greater prominence. Other villages in which there were churches, are Telle

[1] Barradas 1612.
[2] Tombo III 158.
[3] Tam *arasadi* from *arasa*, ficus religiosa.

(Teli), Palicure (Palaikkuda), Curecure, (Kandakuda ?), Tetapule (Tetapole) and Puldevael (Puludivayal).

The Father in charge of Etale "is constantly going from church to church, and in great danger on account of elephants, leopards and bears and hostile Sinhalese who roam through these woods."

GALLE

The Jesuit Residence of Galle begun in 1621 was intended to develop into a College on the same lines as that of Colombo. In 1620 a Jesuit Father from Colombo preached the Lent with such success that the people, eager for a good school for their children, pressed the Superiors of the Society to build a church in Galle promissing to give a site, to pay the expenses of the building, and to maintain the Fathers. But as Galle was not in the missionary field of the Jesuits it could not be done unless the Bishop of Cochin desired it. There was already in Galle a Franciscan monastery with cloisters and dormitories and a church of the Conception, in which the sacraments were administered to more than 2,000 Christians living outside the Fort. There was also a church served by secular priests, and a church of Our Lady of the Rosary of the Dominicans, besides a chapel of the Misericordia. But the townspeople of Galle carried the matter to the Bishop who gave the necessary permission and two Jesuits, a priest and a lay brother, took up residence in the Casa da Misericordia and set up a school.

The Jesuit church of the Mother of God was soon erected on the extreme point of Galle with money contributed by the people. When the Captain-General Constantine de Sa visited Galle he granted a village, at the request of the Disawa, Domingos Carvalho Cao, for the maintenance of the Residence. In this village the Father succeeded in converting and baptizing four adults. In Lent much good was done in Galle with God's grace, by the Father's sermons on the passion. He preached three times a week; on Sundays in the principal church, on Wednesdays in the chapel of the Misericordia and on Saturdays in the Dominican church. In the afternoon he taught Christian doctrine to the children of the school, and at its conclusion the children were taught to sing such charming hymns that it attracted many people. The Father also taught in the school which was in the charge of the Brother.

The Residence of Galle was under the administration of the Rector of the College of Colombo, but there is little recorded of Galle save occasionally the names of the Jesuits stationed there :—

1623 Father Goncalo Paes and Brother Blasius Serranus.

1627 Father Johannes Maria Greco and Br. Bernadino Georgio.

1628 Fr. Simon de Leiva and Br. Luis Cardoso.

1634 Fr. Johannes Camello and Fr. Manoel Martins.

1640 Frs. Louis Pinto and Antonio Delgado.

CHAPTER XII

Military Chaplains

WHEN Constantine de Sa erected forts at Batticaloa and Trincomalie he placed Jesuit Fathers to minister to the garrisons, Father Antonio Soeiro at Batticaloa and Father Sebastian de Fonseca at Trincomalie. Chaplaincies were very hazardous work in Ceylon and not only involved the presence of the chaplain on the field of battle, but entailed the endurance of privations in time of siege and the labour of long marches during the incessant expeditions. The two forts on the Eastern coast cut off the King of Kandy from all communications with foreigners. Senerat, King of Kandy, was at this time attempting to seek the aid of a foreign sea power to oust the Portuguese from the island. When he was baffled in this way, he turned to the Sinhalese chiefs of Colombo and succeeded in persuading some of Sa's most trusted Sinhalese military officers to entice the general to take the field against Kandy and desert him in battle. When the unsuspecting General was thus marching to his doom in 1630, he had two Jesuit chaplains with him, his own confessor, Father Simon de Leiva, and the chaplain of the troops, Father Antonio Pedrosa.

The Portuguese army successfully marched to Uva, and entered and sacked Badulla, whereupon the conspirators deserted to the enemy in a body with their troops, leaving the Portuguese at the mercy of the King's army. The general decided to retreat immediately and fight his way back to Colombo pursued by the Kandyans.[1] In the final encounter at Wellawaya on 24 August, 1630, the General received a mortal wound. Bending over the prostrate penitent Father Leiva was giving a last absolution when he was himself shot with an arrow. In the course of the grim fight for the dead General's body, Father Leiva was killed and beheaded. He was only 37 years old at the time and had not been more than three years in the island. Born in 1593, he came out to India in 1623 and to Ceylon in 1627, and had been superior of the Residence of Galle for two years when he was made military chaplain.

His companion Father Pedrosa, who was the missionary at Matiyagama and had accompanied the army as chaplain to the troops, was also wounded while engaged in his ghostly duties to the fallen men. He owed his life to a Sinhalese soldier who saved him from death hoping to gain the reward[2] which the King offered for taking the prominent Portuguese alive. He was a priest who spoke Sinhalese fluently and was treated with great kindness on the orders of the King, who caused him to be nursed of his wound and honourably entertained, with ample freedom to move about as he pleased among his fellow captives. The money and clothing that the King supplied him, the Father distributed among the needy prisoners.[3]

When the King finally offered terms of peace in 1632 as his attempt to besiege Colombo proved fruitless, he

[1] "Rout of Constantine de Sa de Noronha" by Father S. G. Perera, S.J. (Historical Association of Colombo, July 1929).

Expedition to Uva made in 1630 by Constantino de Sa de Noronha, as narrated by a soldier who took part in the Expedition. Translated by Father S. G. Perera, S.J., Government Press, Colombo, 1930.

[2] Cordara Hist. S.J. VI 332.

[3] Simao de Figureydo, 1643.

sent Father Pedrosa with his ambassadors, entrusting to him a most courteous letter to the Rector of the Jesuit College, in which the monarch spoke very highly of Father Pedrosa and expressed his regret that he was unable to restore Father Leiva whom also he would gladly have sent back to the Society. Father Pedrosa, he added, was released without any ransom, and he asked the Rector in his turn to mediate and secure peace. The liberated priest who had great reason to be grateful to the Kandyan monarch tried his best to promote the desire of the King and did all he could; but a party in Goa was bent on exacting hard terms. The King's ambassadors went to Goa,[1] and Domingos Carvalho Cao who accompanied the ambassadors at the King's request to urge the peace, was so affronted by the Viceroy that the old man, then 80 years of age, took ill and died. The Jesuit Fathers gave him burial in the church of the Bom Jesu at Goa,[2] "because of the many obligations in which he has placed us." His son Pedro Carvalho Cao was a Jesuit.[3] The peace was finally settled on 15 April, 1633, and accepted by Rajasinha at Attapitiya in December.

Father Pedrosa had again the good fortune to escape the fate of another Portuguese army and of a Jesuit chaplain, at Gannoruwa in 1638. In that year he was again summoned from Matiyagama to accompany another ill-fated expedition of the General Diego de Mello de Castro, who set out in February 1638 to invade Kandy, undeterred by the fate of Pedro Lopes de Souza and Constantine de Sa. The army entered the capital as usual unopposed, set it on fire and made for Balana the same

[1] "The Last Tready of Peace between the King of Kandy and the Portuguese" by Fr. S. G. Perera, S.J., *Ceylon Literary Register* III 289 and sqq.

[2] Queyroz 720.

[3] Vida do Ir. Pedro de Basto, S.J. 120.

day. Of all places in Ceylon, Balana was the most fateful to the Portuguese and Nemesis overtook him there. The thick shades of night fell before the troops, worn out by a day's work and harassed by the pursuing foe, could cross the river at Getambe. The General decided to halt. Fighting went on during the night, and next morning, Palm Sunday, the Portuguese found themselves surrounded by a resolute army. This brought the General to his senses and he sent some of the priests to beg an armistice. They had no better success than the Franciscan and Augustinian friars sent to the General by Rajasinha to warn him against violating the sworn peace. The Sinhalese troops deserted and the Portugese were cut to pieces. "On the day when the Church places palms in our hands, the palm of victory fell to the enemy."

Among the killed was Father Antonio Soeiro. Rajasinha's sympathy for Catholic priests was well known to his troops and Father Soeiro was taken alive; but the Kandyan generals did not share the King's feelings towards the priests of his mother's faith.[1] "Why have you spared this arch enemy of our religion?" a Kandyan general demanded. The submissive soldiers repaired their mistake and the Father's head was added to the ghastly pile.[2] Father Antonio Soeiro had long been a military chaplain. Born at Barba in the diocese of Evora, he joined the Society in 1602 and sailed out to India in the following year. He was appointed to the Ceylon mission in 1605 while still a scholastic and learnt Sinhalese with such great diligence that he is described as thoroughly versed in the language. During the first part of his missionary career he was Minister of the College of Colombo, 1608—1611, but was made military chaplain and

[1] Rajasingha was a son of Dona Catherina.

[2] *Relatione delle Missione e Christianita* Francesco Barreto (Roma 1645) pp. 101-3.

was once stationed at Batticaloa. He had seen a good deal of warfare in Ceylon. In 1618 he accompanied Teixeira to Jaffna and reported to the Jesuit Visitator[1] of the Missions the barbarities of that warrior of which he was an eye-witness.

Many stories are told of him and he is described[2] as much given to prayer and penance. During his long career as military chaplain he chose to endure the privations of the common soldiers in order to be more in touch with them. With no other baggage than his mat, which he carried himself, he marched on foot, often unshod like the soldiers, along with the rank and file, and lived on the rice of the *caldeiro* of the soldiers. The general had ordered a palanquin for him, but he gave it to some footsore or wounded soldier. He is said to have slept with his battered hat for a pillow. He was very devoted to his men and in time of disturbances he visited the Christians who were beyond the reach of the ordinary missionaries. But his principal care was for the soldiers. When the army pitched camp during a march, he sought out a quiet spot, far from the officers quarters, to be at the service of any soldier who needed his ghostly counsel. His serviceable hat stuck on a staff marked his lodging. The soldiers came in consequence to have a high esteem of his holiness and had many stories to tell of his piety and devotion. He was even reputed among them for a thaumaturgus, and the soldiers marched willingly to action when he was by. He was 61 years old at the time of his death.

His companion Father Pedrosa was also taken captive but his usual good fortune did not abandon him. He may perhaps have owed his life to the fact that he was

[1] Andre Palmeyro, 1620.
[2] Manoel Sylveiro 1641.

well-known in Kandy. At any rate he gained his liberty very soon, for he was present at the battle of Ambanwela[1] in January, 1639, when a bullet passed through him[2] and he had to be relieved by the Italian Jesuit, Didacus de Sigueiros. When he recovered he returned to his usual work at Matiyagama. Thence he was soon summoned to accompany the force that was going to relieve Galle against the attack of the Dutch forces. In March 1640 when Galle fell, Father Pedrosa was again wounded, captured and taken to Batavia as prisoner of war along with the two Fathers of Galle, Luis Pinto and Antonio Dalgado. All the Portuguese taken at Galle were assembled in the Jesuit house and conveyed to Batavia with the Jesuits. The priests were of great help to the poor captives who were greatly harassed by the Hollanders. The three Fathers were brought back to Galle in the ships *Waterhout* and *Capelle* on 29 May, 1641, as Don Philip Mascarenhas the new Captain-General offered to ransom them.[3] Jan Thysen preferred to exchange them for some prisoners taken by the Portuguese at Negombo. Eventually the exchange was effected.

Father Pedrosa returned to Matiyagama only to meet his death at hostile hands on 8 August, 1643. He was on his way to the Portuguese camp for mass and confessions when he fell in with a troop of Sinhalese soldiers who killed and beheaded him. He was at the time only 42 years of age being born in 1601 at Lavanhos in Coimbra. His career had been a most stirring one. He was not merely an experienced military chaplain and a missionary but a general favourite with all ranks, from the King of Kandy down to the Sinhalese villager. He spoke

[1] Queyroz 810.

[2] Didacus de Sigueiros 1639.

[3] *Ceylon Literary Register* (1887–8, Weekly) II, 6–7, 21, 415.

Sinhalese with fluency having made his studies in the College of Colombo, and was present at nearly all the historic battles of the period.

Father Antonio Pedrosa had been bred a solider and his soldierlike qualities were a great factor in his success. Two of his brothers were Jesuits, and when one of them set out for India, the young soldier determined to follow him. The death of this priest-brother on his way to India affected him so much that he made up his mind to become a Jesuit himself. He was then only 20 years old, and after his noviceship in Cochin he was sent to Ceylon for his studies and attended the classes of humanities in Colombo, where he also mastered the Sinhalese language. In 1628 he was assigned for the work for which his past life had fitted him.

He was much respected by the Portuguese officers, and both Buddhists and Christians are said to have looked up to him as to a father. He had seen many a ghastly sight in the warfare which, according to another Jesuit, had turned this island into a pool of blood. Though he had escaped so far, Father Pedrosa had a presentiment of his coming end. For, just a week before his death, he was in Colombo, having come to the College for the feast of St. Ignatius the founder of the Society, 31 July, 1643. The country was then much disturbed and as he had to go to the Portuguese camp from Matiyagama he knew he was running great risk. Accordingly he prepared for death by a general confession, telling his Confessor that he did so to be prepared for anything that might happen. He had at the time another brother in the Society working in Ceylon.[1]

[1] Annual Letter, 1643.

CHAPTER XIII

The Mission of Jaffna

WHEN the kingdom of Jaffna became a Portuguese Province the authorities became alive to their responsibilities. It is the recognised right of every subject of the king of Portugal to have the gospel preached to him; consequently the duty of the king to provide preachers of the gospel. Therefore the governor of Jaffna, Philip de Oliveyra, and the Bishop of Cochin, Dom Frey Sebastian de S. Pedro, began to take steps to fulfil the duty of their royal master. Unlike other Portuguese officials of the time, Oliveyra was a man of as great zeal and kindness as he was intrepid in the use of the sword. He now threw himself heart and soul into the work of the evangelization of the kingdom of Jaffna, lending it all the aid of his position, the influence of his personality and the resources of his private purse: and in his lifetime he had the satisfaction of seeing almost all the inhabitants of his province receive the Catholic faith. There can be no doubt that the phenomenal success of the Christian mission in Jaffna was due to his favour and activities.

With his support the Franciscan friars accomplished in a short time, on a very large scale, the conversion at which they had hitherto laboured, not unsuccessfully,[1]

[1] The labours of the Franciscans are recorded in the *Conquista Spiritual do Oriente* by Friar Joao da Trinidade. Ms. Vatican Archives chapt. 54—55, ff 845—923.

without it. But it was not enough to baptize those who were ready to embrace Christianity: the people had to be instructed, and proper instruction is not only a matter of patience and perseverance but one that required a thorough knowledge of the language of the people. The Franciscans, however, desired to retain in Jaffna, as elsewhere, the monopoly of evangelization. When some Dominican friars came to Jaffna to help in the mission work, they were requested first of all, to obtain the consent of the superiors of the Franciscan Order to participate in the work. They had therefore to remain idle for eight months[1] till the permission was given with limitations that confined their work to the town of Jaffna. The Jesuits on the other hand abstained from entering Jaffna, though that peninsula was within the mission field allotted[2] to them in 1602. But the necessity of adequate catechetical instruction of the converts made the Bishop of Cochin turn to the Society of Jesus.

"Knowing well" wrote the Bishop,[3] "both from experience and by sight, the care and zeal and assiduity with which the Religious of the Society of Jesus apply themselves to the study of the language of the country in which they are, and the ardour with which they catechize the Christians entrusted to their care,—a matter in which they far excel all other Religious in these parts,"..."We judge it good to ask the Reverend Father Gaspar Fernandez,[4] Provincial of Malabar, to send Religious of the Society to Jaffna." It was not difficult for the Provincial to find Jesuits both able and experienced in mission work among Tamil-speaking people. Accord-

[1] Queyroz 694-5.
[2] See Ante p. 31.
[3] Dom Fery Sebastian de S. Pedro. 11 November 1622.
[4] Provincial of Malabar 1615—1623.

ingly Father Pero Rebello,[1] a Professor of Theology in Cochin, was sent to arrange the preliminaries, which took four months. It was agreed by Oliveyra that the Society should be given a definite part of the mission for evangelization and the Franciscans consented to resign to them the cultivation of the inland parts of the peninsula, one league from the sea, keeping to themselves the missions along the coast.

In 1623 three Fathers, Jeronimo Froes,[2] Petrus Johannes Nocita,[3] an Italian, and Gaspar Leal,[4] missionaries well versed in Tamil. joined Father Rebello, and others were sent in the following years, including Fathers Ignatio Bruno, Pierre de Burgoin, a Frenchman, who were both noted for their literary compositions[5] and Father Robert de Nobili, the famous Sanskrit scholar "who owing to his advanced age and infirmities came to Jaffna from the mission of Madura to rest for two years, during which he did much good with the books he composed for the children."[6] The full complement of Jesuits in Jaffna was 16, and under their indefatigable labours the mission of Jaffna soon became "the largest and the best of all the missions in charge of the Fathers" of

[1] Born 1583 at Ponta Delgada, he came to India in 1602, Rector San Thome 1619, Cochin 1620. From Jaffna he came to Colombo as Rector, and died at Goa 1627.

[2] Born at Lisbon in 1578, he entered the Society in 1596, and had served at Goa and Cochin. He was in Jaffna 1623—41 and was stationed at Mugamale and Pale, was Rector of Jaffna for a short time and Rector of Colombo in 1648. In 1655 he was in Cochin. He is said to have known Tamil very well. Date of death unknown.

[3] Born at Catanzare, Naples, 1580, entered the Society 1598, arrived in India 1610, Colombo (Malwana) 1611, 1620 Rector Negapatam, 1623 came to Jaffna; Rector of Jaffna 1634—7, Rector of the Fishery Coast 1644—46. Died, Tuticorin, 18 April, 1646.

[4] Born 1598, entered the Society 1613, 1623—32 Jaffna (1628 Pandetirippu) 1632 India, Minister Colombo for four years, 1655 Fishery Coast. Date of death unknown.

[5] See Appendix No. 4 & 5.

[6] Costa 1648.

the Province of Malabar, "largest, because it surpasses all others in the number of Christians, the best, because of the goodness and docility of the people and because of the greater care and devotion with which all treat the things of God and of the faith."[1] In the first two years the number of converts amounted to 11,000; in the third year 19,000 were baptized making the total Christian population of the mission 30,000[2] a number which soon rose to 42,812[3] and eventually exceeded 50,000.[4]

In the town of Jaffna the Jesuits had a church built for them by Oliveyra and a College endowed by the Governor with the consent of the Captain-General of Ceylon and of the Viceroy. The endowment consisted of an annual income of 1,600 *parduos* from the revenues of the temple villages of Jaffna wherewith to support the sixteen Fathers engaged in missionary work, to prepare others to take their place, and to employ the officials needed for the task, sacristans, teachers, kanakkapulles, etc. The Superior of the mission lived in the town of Jaffna and was Rector of the College. This College was not of the same kind as that of Colombo, but a smaller institution consisting of a school for about 80 children and a course of humanities followed by twenty-two pupils[5] who were destined for an ecclesiastical career. Besides the Rector there was another Father engaged in teaching and a lay brother looking after the temporal affairs who also served as the procurator of the missionaries, and a virtuous secular priest looking after the school. The two Jesuits in Jaffna had moreover to

[1] Silveyro 1641.
[2] Andre Lopez, 2 January 1627.
[3] Costa 1648.
[4] Lobo 1629. M. de Azevedo, 4 December 1638. (Besse 449).
[5] Costa 1648.

preach, hear confessions and visit the hospital and the prison.

A letter of Father Rebello written in 1625 gives us some interesting information about the nature and the methods of the Jesuit Mission. The zeal and fervour of Oliveyra, the conversion of the higher classes and of the members of the royal family,[1] created a movement in favour of Christianity by which the Fathers profited to the utmost. Churches were erected at suitable centres and the adults willing to be Christians were set first of all the task of learning the prayers. "So quick is their memory that few were those who did not know them all" in the short space of ten or fifteen days. Then the articles of the Christian faith contained in the creed were declared and explained to them along with the commandments of God and the precepts of the Church. When all that was properly understood, the adults were baptized in groups of about a hundred at a time. In the instruction of these neophytes the Fathers were assisted by catechists and teachers "many of whom are very clever in the matter and catechize excellently, declaring each mystery of the faith by some comparisons not less esteemed by them than by the Hebrews."

With the children the work was much easier, because schools were set up from the very beginning, and the children of parents willing to be Christians had also daily catechism classes "whereby in a short time they know the prayers and are baptized." After baptism the children continue to attend catechetical instruction and make further progress in the knowledge of the faith. At Acchuvelly, for instance, 700 children attended catechism class daily, while the secular school had only 140 pupils.

[1] On 18 June 1623, Queyroz 693.

"Rare is the child who does not know some chapters of the catechism by heart, and there are many who know them all, and some who know besides five to six hundred Tamil verses from the Life of Christ."

The instruction of children was the foremost care and the chief work of the missionary, and the success of the Jesuit method of instruction was marvellous. "They are all so well instructed by our Fathers that there is scarcely a boy or girl who does not know the catechism thoroughly, besides the whole book of Marcos Jorge which has been translated into their language."[1] "It is a matter for thanksgiving to God our Lord, to see how well the children are taught, and how well they know the prayers and the catechism and many other things that the Fathers have done into their language......They are all masters and are able to teach the Christian doctrine even to men of advanced age."[2] "It is a matter for consolation to see how the children learn the mysteries of our holy faith and are able to recite the catechism and many other prayers which the Fathers have translated into their tongue."[3] "These children are indeed the best instructed in the whole of the East."[4] That these testimonies are well founded we know from the very person who in after times tried to pervert the children of the next generation, Philip Baldaeus, the Calvinist Dutch minister stationed in Jaffna after its capture by the Hollanders. After describing the way in which St. Francis Xavier first launched his method of systematic instruction of the young and how it was carried on with ungrudging energy, he writes, speaking of Jaffna: "By and by

[1] Figureydo 1643. The Catechism of Marcos Jorge was translated by Father Anrriquez and printed at Punnaikayal.

[2] Andre Lopes 1644.

[3] Annual Letters 1644.

[4] Costa 1648.

came the Jesuits, who in these regions are called Paulists in as much as they were sent by Pope Paul III.[1] They have worked most of all, and in zeal and prudence and tact in teaching the young and attracting the old, they greatly surpassed the Franciscans and all other religious bodies. And I willingly admit that I liked their proceeding and that I have walked in their footsteps in working at the reformation of all churches and schools of Manar and Jaffnapatam, as long as their teaching did not clash with our reformed teaching."[2]

On Sundays and feast days the men, women and children came in separate groups for catechetical instruction after which Mass was said for all. At the Offertory the new Christians came up to give their offerings which were entrusted to one of the chief men of the place to be spent in the service of the church and for the poor. But "rarely was it needed for the poor, for in this kingdom beggars are very scarce, as all live by their labour." After the Offertory the Father preaches a sermon "which is mostly about matters of faith." After mass inquiry is made about those who were absent on the previous Sunday or feast day.

"These new Christians are very ready and willing to perform any service for the church, however humble it be. They themselves fetch the material for the erection of churches and labour at them with their own hands." On great feast days it is the chief men of the village who carry the cross in procession or bear the feretory. At the feast of SS. Peter and Paul, the patrons of the church of Telipole, in 1625, a near relation of the late king of the

[1] The reverend gentleman is mistaken. The Jesuits were called Paulites in India because they came from the famous College of St. Paul, Goa, previously called the College of Santa Fe.

[2] Baldaeus.

country carried the *charola*[1] on his shoulders along with others in the presence of 5,000 people who took part in the procession. After a feast there is always a dramatic representation in Tamil, explaining the significance of the feast or mystery of our faith or an incident in the life of the saint. Many of the churches had permanent theatres erected for the purpose on the church grounds and some of the earliest Christians literary compositions are mystery plays and dramas.

[1] *Charola* is Portuguese for bier or feretory in which an image of a Saint is carried in procession. Hence the Sinhalese for a procession is, in the Christian usage, *scrole*.

CHAPTER XIV

The Trials of the Jaffna Mission

THE success of the Jaffna Mission of the Society of Jesus was something unique, without parallel in India or Ceylon. Practically the whole peninsula became Christian in a few years. The new Christians were docile and devout and the Portuguese officials helped and favoured the mission in a manner that was exceptional. Many a writer has had to resort to fantastic conjectures [1] to explain this phenomenal success. The missionaries engaged in the enterprise attributed their success to two causes, one supernatural and the other natural; to the prayers of the six hundred martyrs of Mannar whom the King of Jaffna put to death, and to the zeal and favour of Philip Oliveyra.[2] The latter is of course the more obvious and tangible and Father Queyroz declares that "it is certain that so many pagans could not have been converted in such a short time had it not been for the great favour with which Phelipe de Oliveyra ever co-operated." [3] But this state of affairs was too good to last and the missionaries were not destined to work long in peace. Troubles came upon them in plenty, from within the kingdom and from without, from the elements and from man, from the enemies of the faith and, worst of all, from the Portuguese officials who succeeded Oliveyra.

[1] See Emerson Tennent, *Christianity in Ceylon*, pp. 7-21.

[2] A. Lopez, 1627. Ig. Bruno 1628.

[3] Queyroz 659.

The first of these troubles was a physical calamity, a terrific cyclone which burst on the Saturday before the first Sunday of Lent, the 20th of February, 1627, and raged with unabated fury till late in the afternoon of the next day, deluging the land and laying low the buildings. The churches and presbyteries in the interior were razed to the ground along with the dwellings of the poor and the lowly, and many lives were lost. A Jesuit Father saved himself from a watery grave by clinging to a tamarind tree and another had to spend the livelong night in a boat stuck in the wood.[1] This heavy visitation showed the nobility of Oliveyra's character, for he was most unremitting in aiding the distressed sufferers, and the personal discomforts endured in this work of charity brought about his untimely death within a month, on 22 March, 1627. He was perhaps the most zealous Portuguese official in Ceylon. A fellow soldier has recorded of him a passage which by a most glaring error some writers[2] applied to a Kandyan general! Captain Joao Ribeiro says of him: "Of this Captain (Felippe de Oliveira) one could write many volumes, for he was no less valorous than Christian and modest, for it is said of him that he never mentioned his father, and that at his registration he entered as his progenitors 'dust'[3] a characteristic so contrary to what is usual in this State where all claim to be descended from the stars."[4]

The death of Oliveyra was the beginning of other disasters. During the eight years of his administration the work of the mission received every encouragement

[1] Queyroz 647-650.

[2] e.g. *Portuguese Era* II 531 N. 22.

[3] Literally "Grass." There were "strong probabilities of his being a person of much higher quality, which his modesty and honour never claimed." Queyroz 623.

[4] Ribeiro *Fatalidade Historica* Bk. 2, Chap. I p. 77.

and support. There was no disturbance in the country nor was it molested by the enemies of the Portuguese, for by a just and equitable government Oliveyra kept the people content and his valour kept aggression at bay. But on his death there began a war and a rebellion followed by the usual tyrannies of the Portuguese officials.

The war was the outcome of the efforts of Constantine de Sa to cut off the king of Kandy from foreigners by fortifying the port of Batticaloa. Rumours of impending war spread throughout the island and there was some reason to suspect that the king was soliciting the chiefs of Jaffna. Alarmed by these reports Lancarote de Seixas Cabreyra, the incompetent successor of Oliveyra, seized the prominent men of Jaffna and confined them within the fort and concentrated all his forces within the walls of the fortress, leaving the rest of the country unprotected. These measures caused grave anxiety among the Portuguese and much resentment among the people. Those Portuguese who were living in the country retired to the fort for safety, and some of the missionaries stationed in the outposts of the kingdom also thought it prudent to take refuge in the fort. But the Superior of the Mission, Father Pedro Paulo Godinho,[1] took a different view of the situation and wrote to the missionaries on the frontiers of the kingdom not to quit their posts. Father Matthew Fernandez of Mugamale was actually on his way to Jaffna when the Superior's instructions were put into his hands. Accustomed as he was to prefer the least wish of his superior to his own, he at once retraced his steps. Meanwhile on the same day Father Bernardino

[1] Born, Coimbra 1589, entered the Society, 1606. 1926–30 Rector of Jaffna, 1630–32 Rector of Cochin, 1633–7 in Europe as Procurator, 1638–40 Rector Tuticorin, 1641–43 Provincial, 1644 Rector Cranganor, died Cochin 2 March 1646.

Pecci who was in the furthermost Residence had to flee for his life under cover of night as a large Kandyan force of 10,000 men under the command of the Atapattu Nilame of Kandy was upon him. He hid himself in the woods for three nights, and succeeded in reaching Pallai the Residence of Father Jeronimo Froes. The two Fathers were taking counsel together when, on the night of 16th September, 1628, the enemy fell upon them. While the troops were busy plundering and destroying the church the two Fathers slipped out in the darkness, but could not keep together. Father Froes being a strong man who knew the lie of the land succeeded in outstripping the foe, and with torn clothing and mangled body reached the fort breathless with the first news of the invasion.

Meanwhile the Kandyans set fire to the church and the presbytery and reduced them to ashes. Then coming upon Father Pecci who, fatigued by a long flight, was unable to make his way, they cut off his head and marched to Mugamale, where they found Father Matthew Fernandez that very night and speared him to death and cut off his head. The Superior in the meantime sent express messages to the missionaries to betake themselves forthwith to the fort, which they immediately did, Father Ignatius Bruno being the last to arrive there on Sunday night. Then the hostile force burnt the churches in the country except the two churches served by the two Italians, Bruno and Nocita, which the Christians "prevailed upon the enemy not to destroy."[1] The church of Karativu escaped also, as the invaders did not enter that island. The Kandyan forces joined by the malcontents of the country marched upon Jaffna, killing on the way two Franciscans, Friar Amador de Madre de Deos[2]

[1] Bruno 1628.
[2] At Chavakachery.

and Friar Andrew, an Englishman. They then set fire to the Dominican church in the outskirts of Jaffna and entrenched themselves outside the fort, while Seixas was forced to look on helplessly.

The two murdered Jesuits are justly regarded as martyrs to Obedience. Father Pecci belonged to a wealthy and noble Italian family of Etruria, which in the last century gave to the church the distinguished Pope Leo XIII. He left Rome for Goa in 1602 and worked for several years on the Coromandel Coast and was at one time Superior of Mannar. In the beginning of his missionary career he is said to have found great difficulty to acquire the vernaculars, but by dint of persevering study he gained such proficiency in Tamil that the catalogues usually marked against his name, "well versed in the Malabar Language," that is Tamil. Towards the end of his life he was smitten with a desire to lay down his life for his faith, and himself asked for the post of danger "and persisted in his request for six months, till at last the Superior consented. Before leaving Jaffna he paid a visit to Christopher Coelho who told him that he would come and see him in his new church some day. 'Spare yourself that trouble' said Father Pecci, 'for the church is situated in the forest and is very far from here.' 'In that case' said the Procurator 'I embrace you for the last time, for you are bent on becoming a martyr.' The Father replied with a smile 'I desire nothing better. I have yearned for it for so many years and have ever prayed that I may be permitted to shed my blood for Christ.' After his death the Procurator related this conversation to Father Pedro Paulo Godinho with tears in his eyes."[1] He was 49 years old at the time of his murder.

[1] Lobo, 1629.

"Older than Father Pecci but not inferior in virtue" was Father Matthew Fernandez. He was born at Cochin and was 64 years old at this time. His learning was ordinary, says a frank historian of the Society, but his prudence was so rare, his zeal for souls so ardent, that he was considered to be one of the most fitted to work among converts and to win pagans to the faith of Christ. After many years labour on the Fishery Coast, where he had distinguished himself by his devotion to the Paravars, he was sent to Ceylon. He was for sometime stationed at Chilaw and was Rector of the College of Colombo for a time. He was then sent to Jaffna, for being an Indian-born Portuguese he was quite well versed in Tamil.

The siege of Jaffna by the Kandyans lasted only thirteen days, after which, on the arrival of an expeditionary force sent by the General from Batticaloa, the invaders thought it best to retire. This was the opportunity of Seixas, who sallied out to pursue the retreating foe, who were attacked but succeeded in escaping with the loss of their leader and of many men and booty. The Jesuit Superior who accompanied the troops had the melancholy satisfaction of coming upon the remains of the murdered Fathers, which were brought to Jaffna with great veneration.

It is characteristic of the Jesuits that they utilized this enforced stay in Jaffna to good purpose, studying Tamil under the direction of Father Ignatius Bruno, who like his countrymen Robert de Nobili and Constant Beschi, had acquired a perfect mastery of the Tamil language. Like all pundits he was not satisfied with the diligence of his brethren in acquiring that language. In his view it was not enough for a missionary to be able to speak the language and preach somehow. A missionary ought to be able to read and write Tamil with grammatical accuracy. In this sense he wrote to the General of the Society, pressing him to give orders to send to the mission only those who are keen on it and have an aptitude for work of this kind. If that is done, he said, it will follow that they will take pains to study the language, "a thing so necessary and so often inculcated by Your Reverence. There is in these parts a great scarcity of those who know the language well, and the fervour of the old Fathers of the Fishery Coast in studying the language is lacking in these parts." Now he had the chance of his life, for the Superior set him to give lectures on Tamil grammar to his confreres, and he reports to the General: "Now that the Fathers of the mission are all here together the Rector ordered that there should be a class of Tamil, a thing which is extremely necessary. I was appointed for the work and I am now explaining to the Fathers the grammar of the Tamil language. All the Fathers are studying with great diligence and fervour." [1]

While they were thus engaged they received the news of the murder of the only Jesuit who had not fled to Jaffna during the invasion, namely the priest of the Residence of Karativu, Father Francis Barbosa. It happened that the Father detected some servants of the house red-handed in a deed of lust. He reprimanded them and administered salutary correction. Whereupon they flew into a passion and profiting by the disturbed state of the country plotted against his life. Choosing a favourable opportunity they fell upon him and cut his throat. When the news of this crime reached Jaffna, the Governor in his indignation had the criminals arrested and brought to the fort where they were tried

[1] Bruno 1628.

and condemned to death in spite of the intercession of the Fathers.

When order was restored in the country the Fathers were able to return to their stations and rebuild the churches and presbyteries. But this rebellion had far more disastrous effects on the work of the mission than on the authority of the Portuguese. The hope of freeing themselves from the Portuguese yoke was the prospect that the Kandyans held out to the people of Jaffna. It was doubtless a powerful temptation to the new Christians, who could not in those troublesome times remain faithful to their religion without being subjects of Portugal. Many accordingly threw in their lot with the invaders regardless of the consequences, taking in some cases an assurance that their churches would be spared. The Portuguese avenged the injury inflicted on them, but the blow dealt to religion could not be so easily repaired. The missionaries, however, did not let themselves be discouraged, and began their work anew, though now they had not the favour and the cooperation of the officials.

In fact it was not long before the favours of Oliveyra gave place to tyranny. The successor of Oliveyra was a man whose callous indifference to the progress of Christianity was commented on by a Jesuit so far back as 1612 when he was the lord of the royal village of Madampe. He was so keen on becoming Governor of Jaffna that on hearing of the grave illness of Oliveyra he rushed to Goa, where by means of his wealth and influence he succeeded in securing that post for himself. An ominous incident at his official entry into Jaffna is recorded by Father Queyroz. "It was observed that while he entered between the guard, the musket of a soldier burst, during the salute of musketry.

with such effect that he was scarcely able to make his confession before ending his life."[1] Under him and his successors the missionaries were forced to look on helplessly while their flocks were fleeced by the greedy officials. In 1643 a missionary wrote, "The oppression which these poor Christians have to suffer is incredible, and is much more than what those of Mannar suffered. I do not know when we shall have redress; but it is certain that for want of it the greater part of the people abandon the territory of our Lord the King, and go to cultivate and populate the lands of our enemy the King of Candia. I wish I could appear before the pious King of Portugal and represent to him the great wrongs which some of his ministers do to His Majesty under the cloak of justice; for I am sure that a King so pious and so desirous of doing good will not tolerate that newly converted Christians find it preferable to be subjects of a pagan king than of his own, on account of the officials who govern and despoil them. The trouble that our Fathers have on this account is very great and their labours are frustrated and brought to nought."[2]

[1] Queyroz, 654.
[2] Figyreydo, 1643.

CHAPTER XV

The Residences of Jaffna

IN the Jaffna Mission of the Society of Jesus there were fourteen large churches, all, except one, of three naves, built at first of wood and mud, but afterwards of coral-stone or brickwork. Most of these churches were capable of containing from four to five thousand persons, and were complete with sacristy, presbytery and large gardens. They were also supplied with all necessary ornaments and vestments, retables, copes, chalices of silver, supplied by the Christians or gifted by Oliveyra or sent by benefactors abroad through the Visitator of the Missions, Father Andre Palmeiro, or by the Provincial. These churches were grouped under 'Residences' or stations at which a priest resided regularly, visiting occasionally the Christian villages and churches. There were twelve such Residences, which, beginning from the one nearest to the mainland and going from East to West, were the following: Kottandarkulam, Pallai, Tampakamam, Mukamali, Achchuvely, Mailiddy, Tellippalai, Mallakam, Pandattarippu, Chankanai, Vaddukkodai and Karativu.

1. The Residence of Kottandarkulam was situated on the borders of the kiugdom of Jaffna. It had seventeen villages with a Catholic population of 2,000 in 1627, in which year there were 200 adult baptisms. In 1644 that number had risen, in spite of the disturbances, to 2538. The patron of the Residence was the Archangel

St. Michael. The district of this Residence was "sandy, unhealthy, without good water and much infested by wild elephants." The priest of this Residence had also to visit the Vanni, "an inland district with many extensive forests of more than ten leagues in circumference, where there were many pagans and about 1,500 Christians, for whose instruction the Father has Kanakkapulles or teachers of doctrine." This frontier residence was naturally a very perilous one and in 1628 the Kandyan troops killed the priest of this Residence, Father Bernadino Pecci.

2. In the same district was the second Residence, at Pallai. Owing to the danger of incursions of the troops of Kandy the church was "strongly built and is surrounded with a high wall with port-holes in the manner of a redoubt."[1] In 1627 there were 2,270 Christians belonging to this Residence, but after the disturbances of 1628 the number was reduced to 1665. The Christian population was spread over five villages, Pullopali, Tammakeni, Alivali, Periapalen and Sorapatu. There was a Tamil school at Pullopallai. The patron of the Residence was Jesus and there was in the church "a beautiful Crucifix, which is a source of consolation to the Christians of those woods."

3. The third Residence was at Tampakamam called by the Portuguese Tambane. The church was dedicated to the Nativity of the Blessed Virgin Mary and was "the largest and the best situated in the whole province" of Pachchilaippalli. In 1628 there were 3,800 Christians, after the revolt 2,500; in 1644, 2,614.

4. The Residence of Mukamali lies "two good hours from Pulopalai, in a wood." Its patron was All

[1] Baldaeus, *Description of Ceylon.*

Saints and had 2,000 Christians living in four villages. At Kilali there was "a hermida of the Holy Cross under the invocation of San Diego. Many Christians and pagans go there in pilgrimage, for God works many miracles, of which it was so far impossible to hold any inquiry for the concourse of people began of late."[1] In the Annual Letter of 1644 a list of miracles is given, and in 1648 we are told that the Holy Cross of Kilalai "works miracles and is much resorted to by a large concourse of the faithful both of this kingdom as well as from outside."[2] It is a place of pilgrimage still.[3]

5. The fifth Residence was at Achchuvely. The church was dedicated to the Holy Ghost and had 4,800 Christians in 1628, in seven small villages, Maravanpulava, Kadduvan, Valalai, Tamplai, Kaitirippai, Navakiri and two others of which the names are indecipherable. The church was "a large and lofty structure, built of coral stone and capable of holding 2,000 persons."

6. The sixth Residence was at Mailiddy where was a church dedicated to Our Lady of the Angels with a Catholic population of 2,590 in 1627, 2,750 in 1641, and 2,985 in 1644. The church was "a large structure of coral stone, roomy and wide, and the house belonging to it a lofty one with a balcony on the top, over the choir, affording a very fine prospect over land and sea, so that it well deserves the name of Belle Videre. It was not above half a (Dutch) mile from the sea."[4] The Christians lived in six villages, Mailiddy, Vasavilam, Palali, Tayidi, Varuttalaivilan and a fishing village on the beach.

[1] Sylveiro, 1640.

[2] Costa, 1648.

[3] See Father S. Gnana Prakasar, O.M.I., *XXV Years' Catholic Progress.* p. 32.

[4] Baldaeus.

7. The seventh Residence was at Tellippali, dedicated to SS. Peter and Paul. It was the chief village of the kingdom of Jaffna and consequently the principal Residence of the Mission with 5,400 Christians and a handsome church, built completely of stone in 1633, when "several performances were given on its dedication."[1] By its side were "certain Scaffolds or Theatres where the Jesuits used to represent certain Histories of the Bible to the people on feastdays."[2] The Christians of Maviddapuram, Vimankamam, Pali Kadduvan and Kankesanturai also belonged to this Residence.[3]

8. Mallakam with a church dedicated to St. Ignatius was the eighth Residence. It was built of plaster and stone and the presbytery was "built upon two arches with a handsome pair of stairs leading to the top of it."[4] Begun after the tempest, in 1641, it was completed finally by the Dutch. The Christians lived in the four villages of Mallakam, viz., Alaveddi, Elalai, Punnalai and Kadduvan, and numbered 1534 which increased to 3222 in 1644. The School was well attended, and the feasts of St. Ignatius and Christmas were celebrated "with great solemnity and devout performances."

9. The ninth Residence was at Pandattarippu where there was "a neat and magnificent church of coral-stone" dedicated to Our Lady of Mercy with a Catholic population of 4,800 in 1627 distributed in six villages, Pandattarippu, Matkal, Sillalai, Periyavilan, Siruvilan and Makiappidy. Here too the presbytery was "built upon arches and had two spacious rooms

[1] Costa, 1648.
[2] Baldaeus.
[3] Costa, 1648.
[4] Baldaeus.

and a gallery, a fine garden and a delicious fish pond or cistern."[1]

10. The tenth Residence was at Chankanai the church of which was dedicated to the Holy Trinity and had 8,500 Christians in 1628 spread over Chankani, Tolpuram, Chulipuram. In 1641 a new church was built of coral-stone, the people themselves bringing the material and labouring at it. The house was of coral-stone conveniently built, surrounded by a wall. Behind the church was an orchard in which was a vineyard and bananas, figs and potatoes. The school was a large one and had 614 pupils "so keen and painstaking in learning their lessons that even when they are driving cattle they sing canticles."[2]

The ruins of this church are still visible, consisting in 1903, of "a nave and chancel." "The nave was divided into aisles by two rows of pillars, eight on each side, of which five on the south and four on the north side, more or less complete, were still standing. These pillars were of brick, and were in circumference, as measured by me,[3] each seven feet six inches.

There were five square-headed windows on the south side of the nave, and four on the north, the place of the central window that should have been on this side being taken by a doorway, also square-headed. There was a central doorway with a window on each side of it at the west end, all square-headed. There was no doorway on the south. The width of the walls of the nave, which were not of brick but of coral-stone, was 4 feet 2 inches. On the inner side of the north door and east

[1] Baldaeus.
[2] Affonso, 1642.
[3] J. P. Lewis, C.C.S., Govt. Agent, Jaffna.

of it was a holy-water stoup of semicircular shape. The length of the nave was 110 feet 6 inches, and the width, inside, 31 feet 8 inches. The width of the west door was 7 feet 8 inches. But the most interesting and the best preserved part of the church was the chancel which retained its roof, vaulted in coral-stone, and was separated from the nave by a stone arch 3½ feet wide. This chancel is a unique feature and both chancel and chancel-arch are in perfect preservation, except that the east window has been broken out or a hole made in the east wall. I noticed, however, that a banyan tree had started just above the chancel-arch, which would soon bring down both it and the roof, if not removed. The length of the chancel inside was 28½ feet and outside measurement 32 feet; the width inside 20 feet. The side walls were 5 feet 3 inches thick, the east wall 3 feet 10 inches."[1]

This church along with other surviving Jesuit churches were handed over to the American mission in 1817 on certain conditions as to using it and keeping it in order, but as the Mission had never made use of it, Mr. J. P. Lewis when Government Agent, Jaffna, recommended the Government to resume possession, which was done. It is now, 300 years after its erection, made an Archelogical reserve.

11. The eleventh Residence was at Vaddukkodai; its Patron the Assumption of Our Lady; Christians 3,800. The church was built of stone and the presbytery was "a lofty house, flat on top, with a pleasant garden planted with trees."[2] Changani, Pandetirippu and Vaddukkoddai, form an equilateral triangle, and all

[1] J. P. Lewis in *Ceylon Antiquary and Literary Register* II 47-50.
[2] Baldaeus.

three churches survived till British times when a Protestant government gave them to the American Mission and were adapted to their purposes. But the church of Vaddukkodai still "consists of an enormous nave and aisles, seemingly under one roof and separated by semi-circular arches supported by massive round pillars over a yard in diameter and ending in plane square capitals. These arcades, I imagine, show us what Chankani and Varani naves originally were."[1] The Dutch finding the church too large for them had cut off a part of the church by a partition wall to form a school-room. Governor Pyl caused some repairs to be made and inserted a tablet stating that it was built by him in the year 1678![2]

12. The twelfth Residence was in the island of Karativu, facing Vaddakkudai. The church was a handsome one of stone dedicated to Our Lady of Refuge. It was the first Jesuit church built in Jaffna and escaped damage during the rebellion. The presbytery was also of stone. The Catholics of Karativu lived in three villages; Kalapoomi, Thenkarai, and Vada Moolai.

The ruined churches still existing are Changanai and Mailiddy. Achchuvelli has been incorporated into the existing Protestant buildings of the place; Vaddukoddai and Pandatirippu still exist as "Portuguese-Dutch churches" namely, old Jesuit churches, modified and adapted to Dutch use.

[1] J. P. Lewis, l.c.

[2] "Doen maken door den Heer Commandeur Laurens Pyl., Anno 1678."

STATISTICS OF THE JAFFNA MISSION

	RESIDENCES	CHRISTIANS			CHILDREN			
					Catechism		Schools	
		1627	1641	1644	1641	1644	1641	1644
1	COTANDARCULAM (St. Michael) ...	2,000	1,600	2,538	200	197	20	
	Vanni ...		1,500	1,000				
2	PALLAI (Jesus) ...	2,270	1,165	1,637	250	208	22	27
	Pullopale ...		720					
	Tamaqueni ...		350					
	Alivale ...		200					
	Periapale ...		140					
	Chirapatu ...		220					
3	TAMBANE ...	3,800	2,500	2,614	300	516	30	45
	The Nativity of Our Lady ...							
4	MUGAMALE (All Saints) ...	1,900	2,000	2,000	200	200	20	25

STATISTICS OF THE JAFFNA MISSION—(*Contd.*)

	RESIDENCES	CHRISTIANS			CHILDREN			
					Catechism		Schools	
		1627	1641	1644	1641	1644	1641	1644
5	ACHCHUVELI (Holy Ghost) ...	4,800	1,701	2,500	440	600	30	50
	Barenporavao ...		178					
	Parenpurnnani ...		215					
	Cateveni ...		350					
	Balalai ...		314					
	Tambale ...		70					
	Caderipai ...							
	Navercare ..		90					
6	MAILITTU (Our Lady of the Angels) ...	2,590	2,750	2,985	314	400	54	90
	Mailety ...		530					
	Vianalao ...		746					
	Pallali ...		536					
	Beach ...		161					
	Thaiti ...		620					
	Velatalevaroo ...		157					

STATISTICS OF THE JAFFNA MISSION—(*Contd.*)

	RESIDENCES	CHRISTIANS			CHILDREN			
					Catechism		Schools	
		1627	1641	1644	1641	1644	1641	1644
7	TELLIPALE ...	5,400	3,414	4,660	669	664	100	200
	(SS. Peter and Paul)							
	Telipule ...		1,173					
	Manituperao ...		590					
	Magamao ...		377					
	Palai ...		231					
	Cathuven ...		307					
	Changanturei ...		176					
8	MALAGAM ...		2,534	3,222	355	500	112	150
	(St. Ignatius)							
	Malagam ...		373					
	Alabati ...		976					
	Ellati ...		763					
	Pugnale Catuven ...		422					
9	PANDETIRIPPU ...	4,800	2,680	2,727	400	375	60	100
	(Our Lady)							

STATISTICS OF THE JAFFNA MISSION—(*Contd.*)

	RESIDENCES	CHRISTIANS			CHILDREN			
					Catechism		Schools	
		1627	1641	1644	1641	1644	1641	1644
10	CHANGANE ...	8,500	2,824	3,140	500	477	114	123
	(Holy Trinity)							
	Changane ...		1,245					
	Polnarao ...		698					
	Cholivaro ...		881					
11	VADUKOTTAI ...	3,800	2,546	2,624	526	250	30	40
	(Assumption)							
	Vaducota ...		1,340					
	Pale ...		1,206					
12	CARDIVA ...	1,400	1,388	1.740	300	227	30	52
	(Our Lord of Good Voyage)							
	Calapume ...	538						
	Core ...	500						
	Valanvale ...	350						

CHAPTER XVI

The Destruction of the Missions

THE Christian Missions begun by the Portuguese missionaries in Ceylon, had, even at the height of their prosperity, a most fatal defect that made for impermanence. They were based so completely on the Portuguese regime and on the Portuguese nation, that the downfall of the Portuguese inevitably involved the entire destruction of the missions. It does not appear to have struck any churchman in Ceylon that missionary work meant anything more than the conversion of the people to Christianity. There was apparently no idea of founding in Ceylon a church that could continue to exist even after the departure of the missionaries. The people of the country converted to Christianity formed only the flock;[1] but the flock by itself cannot constitute a church, which must consist of both flock and shepherds, for legitimate pastors are as necessary for a church as Christians. In India St. Francis Xavier had solved the problem by raising Indians to the priesthood and associating them with him in the work of evangelization. But in Ceylon no one had the foresight to consider what would happen to the thousands of Christians in this Island if political upheavals compelled the Portuguese missionaries to quit

[1] The only two priests from Ceylon were, Don Joao, Prince of Kandy; and Philip Botelho, a scion of the Royal Family of Kandy. They were not in Ceylon as priests. Don Philip Nikapitiya of Sitawaka, a cleric, died at Coimbra; and Constantino de Christo, son of the King of Jaffna was a Franciscan friar in India. (Torre do Tombo, Liv. d. Moncoes 60, 216, 191.)

the country, leaving the Christians priestless and churchless, for the churches in the island belonged to the State and would become spoils of war. This situation was of course not so obvious at the time as it is now, when we look back in the light of recorded history.

This deplorable error was probably due to the fact that no Portuguese, lay or clerical, at any time seriously contemplated the possibility of their being driven out of the Island by war. They had such unbounded confidence in the power of the Portuguese State to recuperate any loss, that it never entered their minds to make provision for a state of affairs which they did not consider to be within the bounds of probability. And yet there was good reason for a prudent churchman to forsee the coming expulsion of the Portuguese from Ceylon. The rout of Diego de Melo de Castro with all his forces in 1638 was not an isolated event. It had happened twice before, in 1594 and in 1630. It did not happen for want of valour or military prowess on the one side, or because of superior forces or armament on the other. It was due purely and simply to want of discretion, to foolhardiness, and to a contempt for the opposing forces that was too characteristic of the Portuguese. They had succeeded in the early days in surviving disaster on the field of battle, because they could be succoured by sea. But since 1602 a growing naval power was cruising about in the Indian waters and increasing so much in strength that it was able to blockade Goa, the very centre of the Portuguese State in the East. But in this island, with a king on land embittered by incessant warfare and an enemy on the high seas gradually increasing in power, the Portuguese had small chance of keeping their hold. The ecclesiastics, however, were singularly blind to the signs of the times

Even before the destruction of Melo's army, Rajasinha, King of Kandy, had contracted with the Dutch to oust the Portuguese from Ceylon. In 1638 the agreement was completed[1] after the Dutch captured Batticaloa, to fortify which Constantine de Sa had risked war with Kandy. In 1639 the Dutch seized Trincomalee and in 1640 Negombo and Galle. All this exposed the city of Colombo, the headquarters of the Portuguese in Ceylon. Negombo, it is true, was wrested from the Dutch for a time, but Galle was lost for good. With it the Jesuits lost a Residence and four Fathers taken in captivity to Batavia. Of these Father Dalgado was brought back to Galle for exchange with Dutch prisoners but held as a hostage by the Governor who threatened to hang him if the Portuguese did not pay greater deference to the Dutch.[2]

At this very time a revolution in Portugal succeeded in shaking off the Spanish yoke. For sixty years the King of Spain held the throne of Portugal and subordinated the interests of Portugal to those of Spain. But in 1640 the Portuguese raised a king of their own to the throne. This new king concerted a ten years' truce with the Dutch, whose hostility to the Portuguese was due to enmity to the monarch of Spain. But the Portuguese in India were not powerful enough to make the Dutch observe the terms of the armistice in the East, and during the negotiations the Dutch recaptured Negombo for good and succeeded in their claim not only to the ports of Galle and Negombo, which they had captured, but even to the districts of Negombo and Galle which they neither captured nor possessed. The result was that the Christians of these two districts were "reformed"

Treaty of Westerwold, Batticaloa 23 May, 1638.
Ceylon Literary Register (Weekly, 1887-8) II 21.

into Calvinism. In the district of Galle this reform was so thorough that the descendants of the Catholic parents became nominal Calvinists during the Dutch regime, and their children afterwards openly relapsed to Buddhism on the advent of the British. In the Southern Province most people retained, till very recently, Portuguese surnames like Silva, Mendis, Fernando, Pieris, Perera, etc., a token that their ancestors were Catholics. But the Christians of Galle were not converts of the Jesuits. The converts whom the Jesuits instructed and baptized were in the Seven Korales from Kammala to Puttalam, and there is not in the whole of Ceylon a Catholic community that kept the faith more faithfully.

The Jesuit Residences in the Seven Korales were imperilled by the Dutch recapture of Negombo, but the missionaries managed to visit their flock and to administer the sacraments even in Negombo, secretly and at night, but the "heretics coming to hear of it, immediately drove out the Fathers publishing rigorous edicts against all priests, especially Jesuits."[1] This confined the labours of the Jesuits to Colombo and its neighbourhood and to the Northern part of the Seven Korales, "which had become almost entirely Christian," at Madampe, Chilaw and Kalpitiya. During the tumults the missionaries were summoned to Colombo. Their presence in the College was so embarrassing at a time when the necessaries of life were scarce that the Rector sent them to India, retaining only three Fathers and two lay-brothers for work in the city. When trouble was brewing between the King of Kandy and his Dutch allies, the Council of Colombo advised the Captain-General to try to win Rajasinha over to their side. Accordingly he sent the Rector of the College, Father Sebastian de Fonseca, along with a

[1] Maracci 1649.

layman to Kandy as ambassadors. But the King could not be moved. He had set his heart on ridding himself of the Portuguese, and kept the ambassadors with him to rouse the jealousy of the Dutch. Father Fonseca was thus in Kandy for three years, ministering to the Catholics there especially to the Portuguese and winning others to the faith.[1] In his place the Provincial of Malabar sent from Cochin a well known Jesuit, Father Bertolameo Bergonco, a man of great learning who knew Tamil, Malayalam and Syriac. But the ship in which he was coming to Colombo was wrecked off the West coast of Ceylon and the Father was taken captive to Kandy. Father Thomas da Costa thereupon became Vice-rector of Colombo, and when the tumults subsided the missionaries were recalled to Ceylon to man the Residences.

The Jesuit Residences were reduced to six, Moratuwa, Weligampitiya, Udugampola, and the Residences in the Seven Korales, Madampe, Chilaw and Kalpitiya. There were six priests in charge of these stations. Nothing is known of their activities except in the case of Father Didacus de Sigueiros, who was in Kalpitiya and was seized[2] by the Dutch and kept in dire confinement till finally he was exchanged for a Dutch prisoner of war in 1656. The vestments and images of the church were seized and taken to Negombo but Father Gaspar de Siqueira escaped. The Christians of the Residences were scattered by the war, and the missionaries were trying to "relieve the unfortunate Christians, longing for spiritual pasture in the wilderness." Circumstances soon reduced the Residences to three. The only Jesuit church that survived the expulsion of the Portuguese was that of Puttalam where in 1690 the Venerable Father Joseph Vaz found the church still standing.

[1] Maracci 1649.

[2] Cardim 1655.

While the Dutch were preparing to attack Colombo as soon as the term of the armistice expired, the Portuguese General, Manoel Mascarenhas Homem, spent the time in shameful inactivity. When the end of the armistice arrived in 1650 the Council of Colombo advised the General to reinforce the garrison of Kalutara, but the General withdrew the garrison altogether, leaving the road to Colombo open to the enemy. He even recalled to the city the garrison of Anguruwatota, Sabaragamuwa and Malwana which ensured the supplies of Colombo. Thereupon, there was great consternation in the city and many began to suspect the good faith of the General. Soon the dissatisfaction spread to the main camp of Menikkadawara and the troops mutinied, deposed their Captain-Major, who was the son-in-law of the General, recalled Gaspar Figueira de Serpe, a veteran Ceylon-born Portuguese, to lead them, and marched on Colombo to denounce the General for a traitor.

The General in his turn was determined to meet force with force and threatened to march the troops in Colombo against the mutineers. The people of Colombo and the priests made great remonstrance, without success. The Rector of the College, Father Thomas de Costa, and Father Manoel Velles went to parley with the soldiers who were encamped at Santumpitiya[1] in Mutwal. The men tried to detain the two Jesuits, but the Rector persuaded them to let him return while Father Velles remained with them. In Colombo every attempt was made to bring the General to reason but he was obdurate. The mutineers would have broken into the city had they not been restrained by the influence of the priests. On 30 November they approached the city gates and the populace headed by the members of the Camara came in

[1] 'The field of San Thome' now Gintupitiya.

a body to the Jesuit College. to call upon the Rector to come out with the Blessed Sacrament to go to the General to intercede for peace. But though the whole city and all the religious begged for it, the General could not be moved. The mutineers thereupon sought to enter the city and slay the General. The priests at the gates of the city made them swear not to shed blood on any account. The General finally gave in and expressed his readiness to retire to the Dominican Convent, leaving the city to the mutineers.[1]

They elected a triumvirate to conduct the government and called upon the Rector of the College to go to Goa to report the matter to the Viceroy and ask for a new General. The Rector declined on the advice of his consultors, but was eventually obliged to undertake the unpleasant task under pressure of the whole city. He embarked on 23 December, 1652, in a transport ship, which managed to elude the vigilance of the Dutch vessels that were blockading the port. But a light Dutch boat espied her and gave chase and captured the heavily laden ship with all on board including the Rector. Father Thomas de Costa was kept in a cruel confinement and died on 26 April, 1654. A fellow prisoner tells us that by a refinement of Dutch cruelty it was only after the Father's death that the fetters were removed from his feet![2]

The deposed General who was sent to India on the arrival of his successor, accused the Jesuits of Colombo before the Provincial, of being the instigators of the mutiny. The Provincial, thereupon, sent his Secretary, Father Joao Camello to be Rector of Colombo and to hold

[1] A detailed account of the mutiny is given by Queyroz, 897—905
[2] Cardim 1656.

an inquiry. The members of the Camara of Colombo, the new General, members of Religious Orders, priests and laymen, all testified that far from being the instigators of the mutiny it was the Jesuits who deserved the credit of having saved the city and even the life of the General.[1] But unfortunately for Colombo the deposed general happened to be the only one present in Goa of the three persons nominated in the letters of succession to take the place of the Viceroy, the Conde de Sarzedas, who died on 13 January 1656; and he was elected acting Governor of the State.[2] This embittered man, now placed in power, made up his mind to wreak his vengeance on Ceylon by leaving it to its fate, a course of conduct of which Father Fernao de Queyroz declared that there was no word in the Portuguese language sufficient to express his detestation![3]

[1] Andre Lopez, 1656.
[2] Queyroz, 906.
[3] Queyroz, 968.

CHAPTER XVII

The End of the Mission of Colombo

IN 1655 when Colombo was besieged the erstwhile Mission of Colombo was reduced to six members of the Society in the College of Colombo, four priests, a scholastic and a lay-brother. One of the priests, Father Francisco Mendes, and the lay-brother, Manoel Borges, apparently left Colombo before the siege began, for no mention whatever is made of them during the siege and they are afterwards heard of in Malabar. The Rector, Father Joao Camello, is said to have died in 1656, but whether in Colombo or in India it is not known. He was then about 60 years old and subject to infirmities. Of the doings of the other three, both Portuguese and Dutch writers testify. Two of them were priests, Antonio Nunes and Manoel Velles. The third and the most conspicuous during the siege, was a Scholastic named Damian Vieyra.

By an act of negligence the fort of Kalutara was lost in October 1655, and the Dutch forces marched in triumph to Colombo destroying the Portuguese forces sent to relieve Kalutara. They were upon Colombo before the city could be prepared to stand a siege. The enemy seized the hillocks commanding the city, on each of which was a church and all of which still bear traces of the names of the churches, to wit San Sebastian, Our Lady of Life,–now called Hulftsdorp because Hulft took his abode and was killed there.—Wolvendaal[1] which is a Dutch translation of a corrupted form of the name Guadelupe in "Our Lady of Guadelupe", and St. Thomas in Mutwal. The manner in which the small band of Portuguese held out for seven months at the cost of sufferings untold and amidst privations the most horrible without ever a cry of surrender, is perhaps the most glorious feat that marked the Portuguese warfare in Ceylon. Whatever we may think of the doings of the Portuguese in Ceylon, however much they may deserve our censures, no one can read without admiration and pity that tale of gallantry and woe. Weary of waiting for a relief that never came, yet hoping against hope, worn out with fatigue and famished, but bold and daring in attack and defence, victorious but without the means of profitting by victory, left to their fate by their countrymen and hard pressed by a relentless foe, plague-stricken, sick, wounded and starving, amidst ghastly scenes, the hapless townsmen held out for seven long months against an overwhelming force of Hollanders and Sinhalese, with a grim determination and an indomitable energy that astonished the very besiegers.

The lot of the Jesuits was indeed a hard one. Themselves sufferers, they had to minister to their suffering comrades. This they did with their customary devotion and charity. Their chief work was the exercise of the sacred ministry. In this likewise they distinguished themselves. The poor had to be succoured, the sick and the dying had to be fortified with the sacraments and rites of the church. Men and women disabled and helpless had to be consoled and encouraged to bear their misery with resignation, and combatants

[1] Wolven-daal, 'dale of the wolves', a translation of *Agoa de Lupe*, a corruption of Gaudelupe.

had to be shriven to face the inevitable death and to be assisted to die well. Nor was this all. More men died than could be conveniently buried. None could be spared to do this work of mercy and sanitation. When no other hands were available the Jesuits with their own hands carried the dead for burial. It was often a perilous task by day under the heavy fire of the enemy, and Vieyra who often attempted it soon gave it up to be resumed under cover of night. As the siege dragged on and its severity increased, the lack of food began to tell on the populace and disease played havoc among the ill-fed and starving masses. This state of affairs called for the utmost devotion of the priests. Cunjee was distributed daily[1] at the door of the Jesuit College, when rice sold at 2500 xerafins a *candil*[2] and the Fathers managed to secure four buffaloes for feeding the starving troops.

Towards the end of the fatal siege when men had fallen and the garrison reduced, it became a matter of life and death to man the defences. The Jesuits as well as the other religious strove might and main to give the defenders every assistance. They shared their dangers, accompanied them in their sallies and stood by them at time of death. They carried arms and ammunition, to keep the scanty defenders well supplied, and when ammunition ran short it was the task of the religious to protect what remained of it at the risk of their lives. They took their turn at guarding and watching, and in time of assault they boldly took the posts of danger, without forgetting their foremost duty of assisting the fallen in the hour of death.

[1] Ajuda Ms. 52-VII-9, omitted by Baldaeus in his translation.
[2] Baldaeus, Dutch text 125, omitted in the English translation.

In such labours there fell the two Fathers Antonio Nunes and Manoel Velles. On 7 May, 1656, five days before the fall of the city, when the bastion of St. John was being scaled by the Dutch, Father Manoel Velles accompanied two soldiers to the fray and when they were slain he retreated with drawn sword. As they soon became masters of that post, some soldiers tried to renew the struggle. Having made their confession to Father Velles the party rushed against more than a hundred Hollanders. There fell "Father Nunes, the Jesuit, a Pattern of Virtue, who signalized himself not only all along on the Bastion of St. John but also in other parts of the city, by encouraging the Soldiers, comforting the Sick, and burying the Dead. He was shot at the Gate of the Bastion with a Musket-Ball, received afterwards a deep cut, and (was) at last slain by a hand grenade after he had killed several of the Enemy with his Musketoon."[1] "During the long siege he was no less conspicuous for his charity and zeal for the salvation of souls than for the valour he displayed when occasion demanded."[2] "He was at the Bastion of St. John during the siege consoling and encouraging the soldiers by Mass, sermons and litanies."[3]

Father Velles escaped unhurt for the nonce and was one of the small band of less than thirty soldiers and *casados*, whom circumstances compelled to take up arms, and who followed the Captain of the city on the same day to attack the woodwork of S. Joao held by more than 500 Hollanders. Father Velles carried the pens and goblets of powder which set fire to the barrels of gunpowder. Many of the Hollanders and their Sinha-

[1] Baldaeus, 774.
[2] Queyroz, 807.
[3] Ajuda Ms.

lese comrades-at-arms were hurled through the air, and the rest were driven out at the point of the Portuguese swords. Pursuing the enemy, the gallant band made its way to the gate which the Hollanders barred behind them. Father Velles thereupon sent to the College for crowbars, but as it was not possible to break down the gate he soon fetched a handsaw with which he sawed the board, and down fell the gate. Eight Portuguese, including the Father, rushed in and were followed by two others. Ten men against an army![1] But the fates were against the Portuguese. A barrel of powder took fire and burnt many fatally. Father Velles "received two bullet wounds, one on the shoulder and the other on the eye brow, and a pot of powder he was carrying on his head broke, but the hat he was wearing saved him from death by fire. During the whole of this action he moved among the flames carrying pots of powder that were brought in baskets. He laboured during the whole of this siege; during the first months at Galbokke and in the bastion of St. Anthony, and finally at Queen's Gate and in the bastion of St. John, where he fell."[2]

The Scholastic Damian Vieyra was not content with a limited field of usefulness. Not being a priest he was untrammelled by priestly duties, and seeing the plight of his countrymen he came forward boldly to play the part of a soldier, and signalized himself by his daring exploits. He was only 26 years old, and seemed to bear a charmed life, for unscathed he came out of many a sanguinary encounter of which he was the hero. Resourceful, prompt and brave to a degree, he was an intrepid fighter, ever in the thick of the fray, himself

[1] Queyroz, 980.

[2] Ajuda Ms. According to another Ms. undated (Goa 31/f. 608), containing an account of the loss of Colombo, dated Negapatam, 29 May 1656, Fr. Velles escaped death.

felling many a Hollander with his trusty sword. In fact he proved to be a far better soldier than Jesuit. He was the only Jesuit to survive the siege but was afterwards expelled from the Society. His services to the beleaguered city were considerable and the courage and ingenuity he displayed won for him the admiration of both Portuguese and Dutch writers.

Captain Joao Ribeiro, one of his companion-at-arms, an eye witness of the siege, says of him: "In the city there was during the siege a Religious of the Company of Jesus, an indefatigable man of remarkable courage. Seeing [on 4th of May] that if the enemy should fire on us from here [the new battery] the city would be open to him in a few days and that he would easily become master of it, as there were by this time so few defenders, [Father Damian Vieyra] invited some of those who he knew would follow him in any enterprise, as they had done in others, and without disclosing what he meant to do, he made thirteen of these promise to be together at midday. Having obtained permission, which he himself asked of the Captain-General, he sallied out at the head of this little band, and entered the battery unpercieved. It was only the edge of their swords that gave the alarm, so that a few alone escaped with their lives. In the space of one hour, which they spent in that battery built of palmtrees and fascine, they set the whole of it on fire, and he and his followers retreated unhurt under cover of the dense smoke, leaving the enemy in amazement and confusion. There is no doubt that if he had 300 men to go with him our good Religious would not have left a single Hollander alive."[1] And again: "It is not possible for me to name or mention in detail what

[1] Ribeiro *Fatalidade Historica de Ceilao*, 197-8.

each one did, but not the least deserving of mention is Father Damian Vieyra of the Company of Jesus for he worked more like a soldier than a professed religious, for there was no assault in which he was not the first, and of many he was the originator, all with success. He it was who faced the 300 that entered by the lake at the first assault; and it was he who destroyed the battery at Queens Gate. In brief I declare that the Company can well be proud of such a soldier and the soldiers of such a Captain."[1]

On 10 May the Portuguese hoisted the white flag of surrender. Three Portuguese envoys presented their terms, the first of which was that "the churches and statues should be treated with all respect; and that the clergy should be at liberty to take with them all things belonging to the ceremonies and all the properties of the church they might desire to remove, the Dutch undertaking to convey them to certain places." The terms were agreed to, but when the Dutch commander saw the ninety three living skeletons that had exacted such terms, he greatly regretted that he had consented to them.

The King of Kandy knew what was the fate in store for the Catholics and caused "Proclamation to be made That all Portugueze which would come unto him, should be well entertained: which accordingly did many with their whole Families, Wives, Children and Servants, choosing rather to be under him than the Dutch, and divers of them are alive to this day, living in Conde Uda; and others are born there. To all whom he alloweth monthly maintenance; yea also, and Provisions for their Slaves and Servants, which they brought up with

[1] Ib. 199–200.

them. This People are priviliged to Travel the Countreys above all other Whites, as knowing they will not run away. Also when there was a Trade at the Sea Ports, they were permitted to go down with Commodities clear from all Customs and Duties. Besides these who came voluntarily to live under the King, there are others whom he took Prisoners. The Portugueze of the best Quality the King took into his Service, who are most of them since cut off according to his kind Custom towards his Courtiers. The rest of them have allowance from the King, and follow Husbandry, Trading about the Countrey, Stilling Rack, keeping Taverns: the Women sew Women's Wastcoats, the Men sew Men's Doublets for Sale."[1]

[1] Robert Knox. *Historical Relation of Ceylon.* 176.

CHAPTER XVIII

End of the Mission of Mannar

THE Mission of Mannar was ecclesiastically a part of the Mission of the Fishery Coast and had no connection with the College or Mission of Colombo or Jaffna, though the missionaries of all three missions belonged to the same Province of Malabar and most of the Fathers sent to Colombo or Jaffna had worked previously on the Fishery Coast and often returned to it. The first Superior of Colombo, Father Diego dé Cunha, came from the Fishery Coast and returned thither after his term of superiorship. It was quite natural that Mannar should be linked with the Fishery. The Pearl Fishery was an Indian affair and the divers of Mannar took part in it with their kinsmen of the mainland. It was the Captain of Mannar who was in official charge of the Fishery. Moreover the people and language were common, and so were the trials and misfortunes. Hence when the Jesuits were compelled by the incessant troubles of the Bishop of Cochin to resign the care of the Fishery Coast, they had also to leave Mannar. That they did not leave Colombo also was due to Don Jeronimo de Azevedo, whom the Bishop of Cochin was unwilling to displease. When the Fathers left Mannar a priest remained at Karisal for sometime without any spiritual charge, supporting himself on the proceeds of a property that belonged to the Society. This also was soon taken away[1] and the last Jesuit left Mannar in 1609.

[1] By the cleric Heytor Fernandez placed in Mannar by the Bishop. See *Vida do Ven. Irmao Pedro de Basto*, 80–81.

The departure of the Jesuits from Mannar was due to disagreements with the Bishop of Cochin which took place at a time when the Jesuits were also odious in the eyes of the Portuguese officials. The Bishop thought that the Jesuits encouraged the Paravars to be disloyal to episcopal and Portuguese authority; the more so as some of the Jesuit Superiors were Italians and therefore believed to be not in sympathy with the Portuguese aims. The blow was intended to hit both the Paravars and the Jesuits, as in fact it did. The rights and wrongs of the matter are of no interest to us now. It is, however, a relief to be able to add that the disedifying spectacle did not last very long, though it did untold harm to the mission. The Jesuits resigned the Fishery Coast in 1608, but in 1611, when the term of office of the Italian Provincial, Alberto Laertio, ended, and a new Provincial was appointed in the person of Pero Francisco, the way was paved for a reconciliation.

This reconciliation was as open and as wholehearted as the rupture, and friendly relations were resumed. But this does not mean that the Jesuits were recalled to their churches. The mission was in the giving of the King, and it was therefore the King's representatives that had to recall the Jesuits: but they were in no hurry to do so. The Bishop's action was meanwhile condemned both at Rome and in Portugal, and the King gave orders (15 February, 1614) to restore the mission to the Jesuits; but royal orders were not much heeded in Portuguese India. India was far from Portugal and communications were long, and the Indian authorities had ways and means of their own to defer unpleasant commands.

Meanwhile the new Provincial obtained from the Bishop what the Bishop could give, and the house and property of the Jesuits at Karisal was given back. The Bishop also gave the Jesuits the needless permission to build churches in the Kingdom of Kandy, and a general pardon to all the Paravars involved in the troubles. This pardon was read out publicly in all the churches in Ceylon. In 1616 this Bishop of Cochin resigned his see and was succeeded by Dom Frey Sebastian, Bishop of Mylapore who was translated to Cochin.

The once flourishing mission of Mannar was by this time little better than a deplorable ruin. The Christians had been neglected, dispersed and untaught. There was no pearl fishery, few priests and little religion, but everywhere was desolation. At last in 1621, thirteen years after the departure of the Jesuits, and seven years after the King's order to recall them, the mission was given back to the Society by Fernao de Albuquerque. The Province of Malabar had in the meantime dwindled considerably and it could scarcely supply the men needed. The Province of Goa came to its rescue; but the Fathers of Goa did not know Tamil and were therefore useless for mission work. Thus only one priest could be spared for Mannar. He arrived there in March 1621 and set to work as the following record shows.

" On the 28th of March one of the Fathers arrived in the island of Mannar. The Christians there had been very much neglected. One of the missionary's first actions was to rouse the people from their apathy by restoring the office of *Tenebrae* during Holy Week, letting them fire off all their arquebuses after the *Alleluia* on Holy Saturday and singing a high mass on Easter Day. Two thousand one hundred persons sought to make their confession. To hear them all would be a matter of weeks. As for catechism they humbly confessed they knew nothing, but were willing to learn."

It was easy to teach willing learners and the good Father seems to have done it in right earnest, for Father Alexander de Rhodes records that when he crossed over from the Fishery to Mannar he found the island to be "full of very good Christians whom our Fathers instruct with great care."[1] The missionary went about the island from place to place, saying Mass on Sundays and feast-days in different churches far from each other, preaching in Tamil and reaping a plentiful harvest at the cost of great fatigues. But he had his consolations too and tells of the great fidelity of the Christians. The feasts of Corpus Christi, Holy Cross, St. Matthew, St. Lawrence and St. Ignatius are mentioned as those celebrated with the greatest solemnity, with long and orderly processions and choirs singing the praises of God.

From this time forward the mission made great progress, but the success of the mission of Jaffna eclipsed all else and the writers of the Annual Letters had little to say of Mannar except passing allusions to the oft-told persecutions. A Portuguese armada arrived at Mannar in 1630 and the only noteworthy incident recorded is a quarrel between the sailors and landsmen. To avoid bloodshed the resourceful Jesuit who was chaplain on board persuaded the officer in command to start on a cruise.

There were generally four or five priests in Mannar, one of whom was Superior of the Mission and "Father of the Christians," namely, the Father who represented the Christians in the courts. Each priest was in charge of a Residence which included two or three churches. He visited them in turn but resided in the principal church which was his Residence. There were at first four such

[1] Rhodes *Divers Voyages*, 30.

Residences, and later five, with ten or twelve churches in all. The following is an account of the mission of Mannar in 1644, written by the Provincial of Malabar to the General of the Society.

"Twelve leagues to the East of Ramanacor is the island of Mannar, which is five leagues in length and about one in breadth. In this Island we have five Residences with five Fathers living in them. One of them is Superior and depends immediately on the Father Provincial.[1] He is at the same time "Father of the Christians" in the name of His Majesty to protect their rights in the ecclesiastical courts as well as before the civil tribunal which sits in the fortress of this island.

Residence of the Lugar of the Careas. The Patron of this Residence is the Apostle St. Thomas: Christians 1200, children attending catechism 120, school 25. This Residence counted in better times more than 18,000 souls, but as the Pearl Fishery was not held in the past years owing to the little favour they found with the King's officers, they were reduced to the present number.

Residence of San Pedro. The Patron of this Residence is the Apostle St. Peter. It has 970 Christians: 150 Children come daily to catechism and 22 to school.

Residence of Totavaly. The Patron of this Residence is the Apostle St. Andrew. It has 430 Christians. These Christians are the first that received baptism in the island in the time of the apostle St. Francis Xavier and from among them were the 600 who died martyrs......... On account of them this island is called the Island of Martyrs.

[1] Which means that Mannar had ceased to be a part of the Fishery and was treated as an independent mission.

Residence of Carcel. The Patron of this Residence is Our Lady of Pity. It has 2,160 Christians: of these 130 children come daily to catechism and 30 to school.

Residence of Our Lady of Good Success. The Patron of this Residence is Our Lady of Good Success. It has 490 Christians: of these 80 children come daily to catechism and 10 to school. Annexed to this is the church of Talemannar at a distance of about three leagues, on the extremity of the island. Its Patron is St. Lawrence. It has 200 Christians: of whom 50 children come daily to catechism. Total of Christians of this Residence 690 Total number of Christians in this island 5450. Children 530."

Some of these churches were richly fitted out. Among the treasures of the church of St. Thomas was an ornament made entirely of pearls, valued at 200,000 *patacas*.[1] When the island was threatened by the Hollanders this was shipped away in a *dhoney* for safety, but was captured by the Maravars.

The few letters relating to Mannar, found in the Archives of the Society record little at this period save the oppressions of the Captain of Mannar[2] and edifying stories of the devotion of the Christians. In 1641 the people appealed to the Viceroy for redress, but nothing came of it. Again in 1644 a Father went to Colombo to report matters to the Captain-General Don Philip Mascarenhas, as the Christians threatened to quit Mannar. The General passed many an order, as they invariably do, to no effect. In 1654 the oppressed Christians of Mannar made an attempt to carry out their threat of leaving

[1] The Spanish piece-of-eight. The name was applied to the rix-dollar. Sinhalese *patagaya*.

[2] Silveyro, 1641. Figureido 1643, Costa 1648, Caldeiro 1654.

Mannar for good, but were dissuaded from it by the Fathers. The Dutch made a descent on Mannar on 18 February, 1654, to intercept the supplies that were being prepared there. They fell upon Aripo and two days later on Mannar. The Captain of Mannar sent two Companies to Aripo leaving Mannar exposed, and the Dutch sacked Aripo killing Christovao de Amaral, brother of the Governor of Jaffna, and destroyed whatever they could.[1] When they made for Mannar the inhabitants fled in terror, some overseas, others to the woods where they awaited events. The Fathers followed the latter and took shelter in the forests. But the attack was unsuccessful and the missionaries returned with the people to find that those who had tried to make friends with the Hollanders had been taken to Batavia for their pains. The missionaries piously thanked God that the deserters were none of their Christians.[2]

After the capture of Colombo the Dutch delayed a while to make their position good, and set out in 1658 to capture Mannar after reducing Tuticorin. Many of the Portuguese prisoners-of-war taken to Negapatam came to Mannar to defend it against the Dutch. But Ryclooff van Goens had little difficulty in capturing Mannar. It surrendered on 22 February, 1658, and the Jesuit Fathers were probably among the refugees who fled to Jaffna by land, there to fall into the hands of the ineluctible Hollandars.

"The sumptuous churches, great monasteries and handsome buildings that the Dutch found on their arrival sufficiently attested the former wealth and prosperity of Mannar. There were seven great churches in the island. These churches were the City church, Totavelli,

[1] Cardim 1656.
[2] Caldeiro 1654. Cardim 1656.

Karisal, Erukalampity, San Pedro belonging to the fishermen, Pesalai and Tallaimannar."[1] These churches were taken over by the Dutch and "reformed" by Philip Baldaeus. In 1697 we find the same churches in use, for Thomas Van Rhee speaks of eight churches of Mannar, "the town-church and one each in the villages of Tutuwalle, Lugar, San Pedro, Carsel, Pesale and Tellemannar."[2] The church of Karisal has been used by the Dutch for some other purpose also, for the ruins of the great church at Karisal, eight miles from Mannar, are still in existence, standing in a grove of ancient tamarind trees and overgrown with banians. "At the back of the church and attached to it is a fort-like building with walls six feet thick."[3] Even after the island was lost the Fathers of the Fishery Coast maintained catechists there to instruct the Christians.[4]

[1] Baldaeus Ch. III 792.
[2] Memoir of Van Rhee 5.
[3] D. W. Ferguson *Ceylon Literary Register* (1886-7).
[4] *Oriente Conquistado* C II D. I, n. 24.

CHAPTER XIX

End of the Mission of Jaffna

THE ruin of the Mission of Jaffna was perhaps more pitiful than that of Colombo or Mannar, because the Jaffna mission was the most successful evangelical work of the Jesuits in Ceylon. The Franciscans and the Jesuits had converted the whole peninsula, and the people had been Christians for about forty years. Another generation of Christians and the faith would have been established more firmly; but it was not to be. Jaffna soon shared the fate of Colombo and Mannar and fell into the hands of the Hollanders in June 1658.

As soon as the fate of Mannar became certain the Portuguese residents rushed to Jaffna with their families overland. The Dutch would have pursued them as soon as the fort was taken, but heavy showers of rain intervened to save and drench the fugitives. We must suppose that all the priests of Mannar also fled to Jaffna with the refugees. But mismanagement hastened the misfortunes of Jaffna, for like Colombo it had not made any preparations for a siege. *Quem Jupiter vult perdere prius dementat.*

The Dutch forces advanced on Jaffna by land and crossed the lagoon in boats almost unimpeded. On 9th March they seized the Jesuit church and College situated in the west end of the town. A few days later they seized the Dominican convent at the other end of the town and besieged the fort. The Jesuits and the Dominicans as well as all other religious and priests sought the shelter of the fort. This fort was a very small one, a regular square, twenty-five paces across. Within were the Governor's house, the Hospital and the Franciscan Monastery. The Jesuit Fathers of the Residences had flocked to the College and the Franciscans who were parish priests in the sea-board parishes of Jaffna had all retired to the Monastery. The cloisters of the Franciscans had therefore to house all the religious of the country who numbered between forty and fifty, according to Baldaeus who was present at the siege.

There was no possibility of escape from Jaffna. A short time before the siege a party of Jesuit missionaries bound for China came to Jaffna to wait for a ship; but the blockade of Jaffna was, even before the siege, so effective, that they had to remain seven long months in Jaffna. At last they had no help but to return to Negapatam in a *Kattumaran*, which consists of four large pieces of timber fastened together. Though uncomfortable and perilous, that was the only possible way to evade seizure by the Dutch. It is said that many of the richer folk of Jaffna resorted to this means of escaping to Negapatam, only to fall into the hands of the enemy there.

The siege of the fort of Jaffna lasted four months and entailed sufferings and privations the most pitiful. But we have no record of the labours of the Jesuits during the siege. There appear to have been eight Jesuits in Jaffna at this time: all eight are heard of in India after the fall of Jaffna, so that apparently no lives were lost. The fort surrendered on 23 June, when it had been reduced to the last extremity. "There was in it by this time no powder, nor water to drink, because the wells were defiled by the mortars and the substance of dead bodies, which was especially the case with the fresh water well that was in the monastery of St. Francis, which was completely polluted by the substance of the bodies of the dead buried in the church and in the grave-yard."[1] "The greatest battle was with famine and pestilence, and the worst that the enemy did was by stones, grenades, and mortars, and for this reason, after the surrender of the praça their Domine (Philip Baldaeus) placed on its gate the following inscription, more worthy of Calvinistic theology than of Ciceronian Latin : *Lapidibus et gratia Dei cepimus hoc fortalicium.*[2]

That the loss of Jaffna as well as the loss of Colombo and Mannar was a punishment from on high for the misdeeds of the Portuguese, was the conviction of all God-fearing Portuguese. Father Queyroz even asserts that the ruin of Jaffna was disclosed "by a notable prodigy, which was well known in India and can be seen from a certificate of Father Thomas Telles, religious of our Society, which summarized, because he relates and affirms on oath things which have no bearing on the present matters, says thus :

I, Father Thomas Telles of the Society of Jesus, testify that, happening to be in the kingdom of Jaffnapatam, in the year 1657 as Vicar of two churches, which were in one of the four Provinces of that kingdom, by name Pachilapali, which is altogether a sandy plain, wherein no stones are found, but which was very thick jungle in certain parts, which are infested by tigers[3] and elephants, one Sunday in the month of July, I heard at midnight three or four bombardments, from the direction of the sea, and a goodly volley of musketry, and immediately afterwards a rattling so extraordinary that it seemed

[1] Queyroz, 996.
[2] Ib.
[3] Leopards.

to hurl the house in the air. Then the servants of the house and outside watchmen, who according to the custom of the churches of that Province were sleeping in the open on account of the heat, came up the stairs and asked me whether I had seen what had happened, and when I replied that I heard, but did not see what it was, because it was already over when I opened the window, they told me in great terror that if I had seen it I should have been awestruck, for it was a thick cloud of fire speeding like a flash towards Candea. On the following day the Sacristan who is there called *Canacapulle*, told me that many had seen that portent and that the cloud had rained many stones over a space of two leagues. I sent the *meyrinho* of the church to fetch some samples, and he brought two, and I kept this one, which I leave in the hands of Father Joao Cabral. This took place seven leagues away from the praça of Jaffnapatam, one year before it was lost: the which I swear to *in verbo sacerdotis*, on this 16th of February, 1666.—Thomas Telles.[1]

According to the terms of the capitulation of Jaffna the religious were transported to Negapatam, except one old Father who was too infirm to move and was therefore left behind. But some of the Portuguese who remained behind and took service with the Dutch were alleged to have conspired to slay the Dutch in church one Sunday and seize the fort. At least, a *topas*[2] or half caste accused them before Jacob van Rhee who believed the tale. Three of the alleged ringleaders "were laid upon the Wheel or Cross and after they had received a Stroke with the Axe in the Neck and on the Breast, had their Entrails taken out, and the Heart laid upon the Mouth.

[1] Queyroz.

[2] Dvi-bashi, "two languages," Sinhalese *Tuppahi*, interpreter.

A certain Jesuit named [John] Caldero, a Native of Malacca was beheaded. This unfortunate person being prevented by Sickness from going along with the rest of the Portuguese Clergymen, had not been concerned in this treacherous Design, much less given his Consent to it. But some of the Traytors having given notice thereof to him by Letters, wherein they stiled him the 'Father of their Souls', he was unwilling to betray his countrymen, for which he paid now with his Head: eleven more were hanged, and afterwards exposed in the open Country on Trees; but the Heads of the Ringleaders were fix'd upon Poles in the Market-place."[1] Baldaeus even gives an illustration depicting this gruesome scene.

It is told of the Venerable Brother Pedro de Basto that on one occasion he prayed earnestly to God to avenge the profaned churches and ruined missions of Ceylon, to which he received answer: "Pedro, pray not so; Ask not for their chastisement but pray rather that they may have the grace to be converted to the Catholic faith." And the Voice went on to assure him that the Hollanders were only an instrument in the hands of God for the punishment of the Portuguese in India, and would, in their time, melt away as salt in water. And such indeed has been the case. The Portuguese and the Dutch have passed away, but the Faith of Christ preached by the Catholic missionaries, though tried in the crucible of persecution, still flourishes vigourously under British rule.

For with the surrender of Jaffna the career of the Portuguese ended in Ceylon, and the victorious Dutch started a campaign of ruthless persecution. All Catholic churches were seized and "reformed" or turned to

[1] Baldaeus *Ceylon* Eng. Trans. 798—9.

profane use: Catholic priests were transported and the Catholic religion proscribed as the religion of the Portuguese. On 19 September, 1658, a proclamation was issued forbidding, on pain of death, the harbouring or concealing of a Catholic priest: all acts of Catholic worship were declared to be crimes; Catholics were compelled to baptize, marry and bury, according to the rites of the Dutch Kirk and to send their children to the proselytizing schools set up by the Dutch: and most powerful inducements to apostacy were held out to the Catholics. Many new converts doubtless succumbed to the temptation and became nominal Dutch Christians, or relapsed to the religion of their ancestors. Others fled from the persecution and migrated to the territories of the King of Kandy and founded the Catholic communities of Sitawaka, Ruwanwella, Kendangamuwa and Ratnapura on the southern frontiers of the Kingdom, and Galgamuwa on the Eastern, and of Weudda, Narangoda, Kandy and Wahakotte in the highlands. Those who remained in Dutch territory could practise their religion only in the utmost secrecy. Neither those who fled nor those who remained had churches or priests, and there was neither the consolation of the sacraments for the old nor books of the instruction for the young. However, as Sir Emerson Tennent expressed it: "Notwithstanding every persecution, the Roman Catholic religion retained its influence, and held good its position in Ceylon. It was openly professed by the immediate descendents of the Portuguese, who had remained in the island after the conquest of the Dutch; and in private it was equally adhered to by large bodies of the natives, both Sinhalese and Tamils, whom neither corruption nor coercion could induce to abjure it."[1]

[1] "Christianity in Ceylon" p. 42.

This state of affairs lasted about four decades when God inspired a holy priest, the Venerable Father Joseph Vaz, to come of his own accord to the rescue of the Catholics of Ceylon. For nine long years he laboured single handed,—the only priest in the island,—living in the Kandyan country but visiting every part of Ceylon in disguise, with a price upon his head. By earnest appeals to his brethren in Goa he soon succeeded in persuading a gallant band of Indian priests of the Congregation of the Oratory of Goa to join him in his efforts to raise up a new church out of the ashes of the old.[1] The Catholic Church in Ceylon which he thus revived, is, today, in the year of grace 1940, an Ecclesiastical Province consisting of an Archbishop of Colombo and five suffragon Bishops of Jaffna, Kandy, Galle, Trincomalie and Chilaw.

[1] Cf. Ch. VI and VII ('The Ven. Father Joseph Vaz'—'The Missionary methods of Father Vaz') and Ch. XII ('The Oratory of Goa' in *Historical Sketches* by Father S. G. Perera, S.J.

CHAPTER XX

Jesuit Captives in Kandy

FOUR members of the Society of Jesus, three priests and a lay brother, were detained in a long captivity by Rajasinha and died in Kandy at different times. The first to be taken was Father Bertolameo Bergonco and a lay-brother novice named Lourenco Carreiro, who were taken together in 1648. Before the end of the year Father Joao de Carvalho, who had been successively Rector of Negapatam, Superior of Mannar and Rector of the College of Jaffna, was taken on his way to Colombo from Jaffna. The fourth was Father Antonio de Fontes who had laboured as a missionary in Cochin-China and Tonquin for 24 years and who fell into captivity between 1648 and 1652 under circumstances of which there is no record.[1] We only know that he was a captive in Kandy up to 1655.

Of these four unfortunate Jesuits the first to fall into captivity and the last to die was the most prominent of them all, Father Bertolameo Bergonco one of the most erudite members of the Malabar Province of the Society, an accomplished student of Tamil, Malayalam and of the liturgical language of St. Thomas' Christians, Syriac. Born at Genoa in 1593, he entered the Society in 1612 at the age of 19, and after his studies and ordination to the priesthood, left for the Indian missions in

[1] Born 1590, he was about 60 when captured.

1623. Soon after his arrival in Goa he wrote, on 28th January, 1624,[1] about the renunciation of his paternal property which he had forgotten to do in legal form in the hurry of his departure. He had, however, arranged with his brother, Francisco Bergonco of Taggia, a place two leagues from St. Remo, to give one thousand *cruzados* a year to the Jesuit Residence of St. Remo, out of his share of the paternal inheritance. He asked the Superior of St. Remo to recover it regularly and spend it on any charitable work of the Society in Europe or India. The property was to remain with his brother unless he died without issue, in which case it was to go to the Residence of St. Remo. It was only after his arrival in India that he made his final vows.[2]

Father Bergonco was soon appointed Vice-Rector of Quilon (1624–1628), where he acquired the Tamil language; then Vice-Rector of Cranganor where he studied Malayalam and Syriac which was found necessary for the instruction of the Seminarists of the St. Thomas' Christians. He was also Professor of Moral Theology; and with the facility he had gained in reading and writing two languages currently spoken in the country, he had a successful missionary career of 18 years, when circumstances made the Provincial of Malabar choose him to be Rector of the College of Colombo.

The previous Rector of Colombo was Father Sebastian de Fonseca,[3] who was sent to Kandy about 1645 at

[1] Jesuit Archives, Goa 9 f. 80.

[2] Another letter of his, (Seira 23 Jan. 1629), exists in the Archives (Goa, 18 ff. 108–9), but it is a business letter and contains no personal details.

[3] Born at Lisbon 1598, entered the Society 1613, came to India 1624, and became Rector of Bengal, Professor of Theology in the Seminary of Cochin, Rector of Quilon, Socius to the Provincial, Master of Novices. In 1628 he was chaplain at Trincomalee, 1644–48 Rector of Colombo, (1645–1648 Portuguese Ambassador at Kandy), 1655 Rector of the Fishery, 1659 Rector Cochin.

the request of the Viceroy as one of the two Portuguese ambassadors to arrange the terms of peace with Rajasinha. That monarch was showing signs of falling out with the Dutch allies, and the Council of the Captain-General of Colombo urged the Viceroy to make peace with Kandy. But Rajasinha could not be moved. He kept the Portuguese envoys at Kandy for three years amusing himself by confronting them with the Dutch ambassadors and exciting the mutual jealousy of the two candidates for his favour. Meanwhile the term of Father Fonseca's rectorship was over, and as there was no knowing when he would return to Colombo, the Provincial decided to send another Rector in his stead. He had been asked by the Viceroy to send to Colombo a person of great consideration, and he hit upon Father Bergonco.

The new Rector set sail in a galliot along with a lay-brother novice Lourenco Carreiro, but their ship was caught in a storm in the Gulf of Mannar and dashed one night against the Northwest coast of Ceylon where it was wrecked. It was the custom of the kings of India and Ceylon to claim the cargo of all wrecks off their coasts. Accordingly men of the king of Kandy not only seized the cargo of the ship but also Father Bergonco and his companion who were brought before Rajasinha. By that time the King had given leave to Father Fonseca and the other ambassador[1] to return to Colombo but they were not yet sent.

Father Bergonco had speech with Rajasinha, who, as is well known, spoke Portuguese with ease and wrote all his letters, even to the Dutch, in Portuguese. The

[1] Don Jeronimo de Azevedo, not the Capt.—General of that name, but a namesake, the son-in-law of one of the richest men in India, Lancarote de Seixas Cabrera.

king was quite pleased with the Father and promised to set him soon at liberty, but put off his departure especially as he had come to know that the Father knew nine[1] languages. Rajasinha said he had need of the Father's services in matters of state, for which reason he would not treat him as a captive but would leave him free to live in his religion and wear his habit.[2] But the old king was wont to forget his promises, for according to information sent to Cochin the Provincial wrote to Rome; "As these promises proved false, for in spite of them the Father was kept a captive, I do not know whether he will ever come out of his captivity, and I even doubt whether the King will send Father Fonseca since he has deferred his departure also. Such is the character of that king."[3]

Father Fonseca however returned to Colombo and from Colombo he went to the Fishery Coast. The Provincial, meanwhile, appointed an acting Rector, and decided to send another Rector to Colombo if Father Bergonco was not released. As he was not released the Provincial appointed Father Joao Carvalho the Rector of Jaffna to Colombo. Father Carvalho set out with a servant but both fell into the hands of Kandyans. Of this servant's proceedings we are told the following:

"A youth of Jaffnapatam, who is in the service of the Fathers (who are prisoners in Candia), gave a noble example of the teaching and formation he received from the Fathers. With blandishments and promises the king himself tried to induce him to abandon his beads, but he remained firm, boldly asserting that they were

[1] Latin, Greek, Hebrew, Italian, Portuguese, Tamil, Malayalam, Syriac, and probably French.

[2] Ignatio Bruno, 29 Sept. 1649.

[3] Ib.

the mark of his religion and that he would not part with them as long as he lived. Further, when the monarch pressed him to come and serve him in the royal palace, the youth spurned the favour saying that he would never of his own accord abandon the Fathers with whom he would rather die than live in safety amidst the pleasures of the Court. The king himself admired the young man's loyalty. *Apud hostes scilicet parit etiam admirationem constantia, praetio habetur virtus*."[1]

Father Bergonco managed to send news of his capture to Cochin whence the Provincial wrote: "I had letters from the Fathers of Candia in which Father Bertolameo Bergonco wrote to me that the King of Kandy was determined not to give liberty to him or to his companion who is a lay-brother novice. I have sent orders recommending this matter to the prayers of the whole Province. In this College in particular they say Mass for that intention and do extra penances. According to the affairs and customs of the king of Kandy Father Bertolameo Bergonco will come out of his captivity but slowly, unless God intervenes with his powerful arm. I have had recourse to divine aid, and now I am seeking human means also by obtaining letters of the Prince of Matale,[2] brother of this king of Kandy, begging for the liberation of the Father and his companion. This Prince is a Christian and now in Goa. I have already written to the Father Provincial (of Goa) to undertake this business. May God Our Lord deign to restore the Father to us, for this Province is in great need not only

[1] Joao Caldeira, 15 Dec. 1654.

[2] Vijayapala, second son of Senerat and Dona Catherina, a somewhat inconstant Prince, who quarrelled with his brother Rajasinha, went over to the Portuguese, tried to communicate with the Dutch (Dagh Register 225–8) was sent to Goa where he arrived 26 March 1643, and was baptized on 8 Dec. 1646. He died at Goa in 1654.

because of the quality of his person but also because of the lack of subjects. I am now appointing to Colombo another Rector, Father Marcal de Leiva who will be Vice-Rector but will wait two or three months to see if Father Bertolameo Bergonco will be set free, for Father Marcal de Leiva is there in the College and is one who can remain for the present. As soon as the winds are favourable for the voyage I will send another, and it will be the one whom the consultors point out, because for that post we need a person of great consideration as the Viceroy pointed out to Your Paternity, whom I beg for the love of Jesus Christ to come to the aid of this Province which is just now in great need of subjects of whom there is lack for administration as well as for mission work."[1]

From Rajasinha's correspondence with the Dutch we learn that Father Bergonco actually delivered a letter of the Prince of Matale to the King. For on 19 September Rajasinha sent from Badulla to the Governor Kittensteyn "the copy of a letter which the Rector Bartholomew Bergoncio presented to this imperial court."[2] In a letter of 1 September, which is not now in the Archives having been pilfered thence, but which ultimately found its way to the British Museum, (MSS 9380) Rajasinha gives information about the letter. He says "On Monday, the 26 of August at eleven o'clock at night there reached me[3] a courtier with two other persons of Goa, who brought me a letter in great secrecy, written in the Tamil (Malabar) language, from King Vigiapala done on the 15th of the moon of March of this present year of (1652)."[4]

[1] Manoel de Souza, 30 Dec. 1649.

[2] Dutch Archives. Rajasinha's letters No. 11. Translation of Ferguson, Journal R.A.S. 55 p. 212.

[3] At Badulla.

[4] Translation of Ferguson, Journal R.A.S. 62 p. 262.

In this letter Vijayapala does not seem to have pleaded for Fr. Bergonco with any great insistence but for himself. He asks his brother to make war on the Portuguese so that they may abandon the idea of taking him to Portugal. At least neither Rajasinha nor Kittensteyn whose comments on the letter are given by Valentyn,[1] make any mention of the poor Father. At all events no further reference to him is found either in the contemporary documents or in the Jesuit letters. Father Bergonco was thus left to pine away in captivity. Up to 1655 all four Jesuits are marked in the catalogues of the Society as "Captives in Candy." After that date the Province of Malabar was so sorely tried that the captives are not even mentioned.

But Robert Knox, an English prisoner in Kandy, trepanned with his father and sixteen other Englishmen at Kottiar in April 1660, met Father Bergonco in the course of his nineteen years' captivity in Ceylon. In his *Historical Relation of Ceylon*, written after his escape, he says, the other priests were "all deceased excepting Vergonse before my time."[2] Father Bergonco he met probably in 1664 when he was summoned to Kandy. Knox has something to tell us about Father Vergonse, as he calls him, and that something is very interesting as it gives us a glimpse of the fate of the old Father.

First of all Knox tells us a story of Father Bergonco and the English seamen of the *Persia Merchant*, thirteen of whom were seized at Kalpitiya in 1657 much in the same way as the Father. "There was at that time an old Portuguese Father, Padre Vergonse by name, living in the City."[3] When the men were brought before

[1] Ceylon, 137.
[2] Knox, 189.
[3] Ib. 133.

Rajasinha the king placed them "in the City of Candy and each of them had a new Mat given them to sleep on, and their Diet was Victuals dressed and brought them twice a day from the King's own Palace." "This civil Reception upon their first coming up into the City put these *Persia Merchant*-men in hope, that the King would give them their liberty." With Father Bergonco therefore "they discoursed concerning the probability of their Liberty, and that the favours the King had shewn them seemed to be a good sign of it: but he told them the plain truth, that it was not customary there to release white Men. For saying which, they railed at him, calling him Popish Dog and Jesuitical Rogue, supposing he spoke as he wished it might be. But afterward to their grief they found it to be too true as he told them."[1]

The *Persia Merchant* men had excellent "entertainment according to the poor condition of the country. Yet notwithstanding, being not used to such short Commons of Flesh, tho' they had Rice in abundance, and having no Money to buy more, they had a desire to kill some Cows that they might eat their Bellies full of Beef, but made it somewhat a point of Conscience, whether it might be lawful or not, to take them without leave. Upon which they apply themselves to the old Father abovesaid, desiring him to solve this Case of Conscience. Who was very ready to give them a Dispensation. And told them, That forasmuch as the Chingulayes were their Enemies and had taken their Bodies, it was very lawful for them to satisfie their Bodies with their Goods. And the better to animate them in this design, bid them bring him a piece, that he might partake with them. So being encouraged by the old

[1] Knox, 133.

Father, they went on boldly in their intended Business."[1] Speaking again of the white Prisoners in Kandy Knox says elsewhere :

"Nor have there been any, I ever heard of, that came to their Temples upon any Religious account, but only would stand by and look on; without it were one old Priest, named Padre Vergonse, a Genoez born, and of the Jesuits order who would go to the Temples and eat with the Weavers[2] and other ordinary People of the Sacrifices offered to the Idols; but with this Apology for himself, that he eat it as common Meat and as God's Creature and that it was never the worse for their Superstition that had past upon it. But however this may reflect upon the Father, another thing may be related for his Honour. There happened two Priests to fall into the hands of the King; on whom he conferred great Honours; for having laid aside their Habits they kept about his Person and were the greatest favourites at Court. The King one day sent for Vergonse, and asked him, if it would not be better for him to lay aside his old Coat and Cap, and to do as the other two Priests had done, and receive Honour from him. He replied to the King, That he boasted more in that old Habit and in the Name of Jesus than in all the honour that he could do him. And so refused the King's Honour. The King valued the Father for this saying."[3]

Finally we learn from Knox that Father Bergonco "died in his Bed of old Age." "He had a pretty Library about bim," "about Thirty or Forty Books, which the

[1] Ib. 133-4. This story is from the sailors' point of view, and not exactly as the Father would have reported.

[2] Apparently the poor Father was left to his own resources for his food.

[3] Ib. 189.

King, they say, seized on after his Death and keeps."[1] Father Bergonco was 72 in 1664 when Knox first met him. How much longer he lived cannot be ascertained. Knox set out on the journey that ended in his escape, on 22 September, 1679, and as Father Bergonco was dead by that time, he must have died about the age of eighty. R. I. P.

[1] Ib.

APPENDIX

Literary Works of Jesuits in or about Ceylon

1. ALVAREZ CASEIRO, VINCENTIUS (1581-1634) born Surrentina, Italy, joined the Society in 1598, was at Cochin 1610--1622, became Rector of the College of Colombo 1622—1624, and wrote:

SUMMA LUSITANA.........ex vulgari in latinum conversa per R. P. Vincentium Alz.

On the title-page of a copy of this work is written;

"Philippus Baldaus V. D. M. in India Orientali
de spoliis Jaffnapatam me possidet
in Jaffnapat. 6 April, 1658."

As the fort of Jaffna surrendered only on 23 June 1658, the book must have been taken when the Jesuit College and church were seized at the beginning of the siege.

2. ANRRIQUEZ, ANRRIQUE[1] (1520—1600), entered the Society on 8 October, 1545, and set out for India in 1546. After two years in Goa he was sent to the Fishery Coast where he lived and died, having been Superior for 51 years. He was in Mannar, 1561—1564, and died at Punnaikayal on 22 February 1600, at the age of 80, and was buried in the church of Our Lady of Snows, Tuticorin.

[1] This is how he signs his name in his letters. He is often spoken of as Henriques, Enriquez.

He was the first European to master the Tamil language[1] which he began to study on the recommendation of St. Francis Xavier. While he was in Mannar he was engaged in the composition of

1. A Tamil Grammar and
2. A Vocabulary for the use of Missionaries. He also translated into Tamil,
3. The Christian Doctrine of Marcos Jorge, adding to it a method of instruction by question and answer,
4. A Method for Confession and
5. A Life of Saints

besides other works. All his books were printed at Punnaikayal from type cast on the spot by a lay-brother.

While at Mannar he also laboured to revise some Tamil Canticles composed by a Tamil Christian of Colombo under the inspiration of Friar John de Villa de Conde, the Guardian of the Franciscans in Colombo.

Many of his letters, including four written from Mannar (19 December 1560 ; 8 January, 14 and 30 December 1561) have been published in Europe and translated into various languages. A copy in Tamil of his " Vitae Christi Domini, Beatissimae Virginis et aliorum Sanctorum " sent to Rome in 1602 is now in the Bibliotheca Vaticana.

3. BARRADAS, MANOEL (1572—1646) entered the Society as a priest at Coimbra and set out for the Indian Missions. He was Socius of the Provincial and visited Ceylon in 1612. His "Description of Ceylon" written on that occasion, describing Colombo, Moratuwa, Negombo, Matiyagama, Madampe, Chilaw, Munnessaram,

[1] See *Um Missionairo Modelo e Linguista* in *O Oriente Portuguez* III 252—259 and a *Bulletin of the School of Oriental Studies* III 144.

Kalpitiya, Maripo and Mannar, has been printed in the *Historia Tragico-Maritima* I (1735) pp. 221—307. It was translated into English by D. W. Ferguson in the *Ceylon Literary Register* IV (1896) pp. 130—135, 155—159.

Father Barradas wrote several memoirs regarding Father Robert de Nobili and the annual letters of 1613, 1615—1617, and 1619. In 1623 he left for Abyssinia and wrote some Memoirs on that country. He returned to India and became Provincial in 1644 at the age of 72.

4. BERGUIN, PIERRE, (1592—1651) a Frenchman, born at Deon (Langres) entered the Society in 1609, and coming to India served first at Cochin and afterwards in Jaffna and Colombo. He was well versed in Tamil and Sinhalese and in 1645 he composed,

Arte e Grammatica de lingoa Chingala,

for the use of missionaries in Ceylon "composed in the year 1645 by Father Pedro Borgoim." Two manuscript copies of the work are in existence, one in Jena and the other in the Berlin Academy. According to the former the book is divided into three parts, the first containing 6 chapters, the second 15 and the third 5. He is said to have composed several other works.

5. BRUNO, IGNATIUS (1576—1659), born at Bagnali in the diocese of Nocera, Italy, entered the Society in 1599 and came to India in 1603. He was in the Colombo Mission, 1608—11, in the College 1608, 1610—11, and at Kalpitiya in 1609. Returning to India he was at San Thome, 1619—20, Fishery Coast 1623 when he was sent to Jaffna, 1624—1633, being stationed at Mailatti in 1628. From 1633 to 1638 he was Rector of Malacca and returning to Ceylon he was at Mannar in 1638, Jaffna 1644—1646 and worked at Vaddukoddai. He was made Provincial of Malabar, 1646—1650, after which he was

Rector of Cochin and died in 1659 at the age of 83, having been 60 years a Jesuit and 57 years a missionary.

He was a keen student of Tamil which he knew so thoroughly that he taught it to others, and greatly promoted its study in the Society. He had written "several useful books which help conversion."[1] In his letters to the General he speaks of a *Vocabulary* he had composed which was awaiting publication.

6. COSTA, MANOEL DE, (1590—1626) was a Colombo-born Portuguese educated in the Jesuit College, Colombo. He entered the Society in 1608 and after his priestly studies was ordained in Colombo in 1620. He died on 15 July 1626. He is the author of the first Sinhalese Grammar composed in a foreign tongue. It was entitled *Ars Chingalensis Linguae,* and was never printed, but used obviously by his fellow missionaries. According to the Annual Letter of 1626, which mourns his untimely death, he had also made many translations into Sinhalese.

7. DYAS, ANTONIO, (1525—1576) a Portuguese who joined the Society as a lay-brother at the age of 25 and set out for India in 1551. In 1552 he accompanied Father Manoel de Moraes to Colombo and returned with him to Goa in 1553. Then he went to Japan, but returned to Goa and begged to be priested, which was done in 1566, after which he laboured on the Fishery Coast chiefly at Cape Comorin, where he died in 1576.

When he was in Colombo he wrote a letter to the Fathers of Coimbra describing the state of Colombo and Kotte, dated, Colombo, 15 December 1552. A translation made from a photo-stat copy of this letter appeared in the *Ceylon Literary Register* III (1934—1135) pp. 509—519.

[1] Jean Maracci, *Relation*, Paris 1651, p. 62.

The original text is printed in Schurhammer, *Ceylon* 639–659.

8. MAYA, SEBASTIAM DE, (1598—1664) born at Lisbon, entered the Society in 1613, and came to India in 1637 after he had been Chancellor of Evora. He was in the Madura Mission and laboured with Father Robert de Nobili. In 1643 he went to Jaffna for his health and was Rector for a year. Afterwards he worked both in China and Japan and was Rector of Macao, Provincial and Visitator of the Missions, and died at Macao, 16 June, 1664.

In 1645 he composed a book entitled *India Christiana*, a work of moral theology for the Indies. It is now in the Vittorio Emmanuele Library, Rome (Gesuitici n. 1549 (3678).

9. MORAES, MANOEL DE, (1521—1553), born at Braganza in 1521, entered the Society at Coimbra in 1545 and set out for India in 1551. In 1552 he was sent to Colombo at the request of the Viceroy Noronha to effect the conversion of the boy-king afterwards Don Joao of Kotte. He laboured for a year in Colombo and Kotte and returned ill to India in 1553 and died there that year.

From Colombo he wrote a letter to the brethren in Coimbra giving an account of Ceylon (Colombo 28 November, 1552). This letter appeared in a Latin Translation in the *Selectae Indiarum Epistolae* (1887) 143—9 and in an English summary in the *Ceylon Antiquary* I 223—4. The full text is printed by Schurhammer, *Ceylon* 622—635.

Another letter of his describing his voyage to India 1551 has been published in *Imagem da Virtude de Coimbra*.

10. PELINGOTTI, LUIS MATTHEUS, (1579–1616) born at Sorbolongi in Italy, entered the Society in 1603 and was sent to India in 1605. Being sent to the Ceylon Mission he was at Puttalam (Residentia Alevichensi) in 1609 and afterwards at Malwana and Matiyagama where he was killed on 6 December 1616.

He studied Sinhalese at Malwana and with the help of an old Sinhalese *pundit* of 70, whom he converted, he composed in Sinhalese,

1. 26 Lives of Saints
2. A Catechism
3. Passion of Our Lord
4. Seven Sacraments
5. Some prayers

and 'many other things in that language.'

11. QUEYROZ, FERNAO DE, (1617–1688) born at Canavezes near Amarante, Portugal, entered the Society in 1631 and set sail for India in 1635. After his studies he became successively, Vice-Rector of Diu, Rector of Thana and Bassein and was nominated Patriarch of Ethiopia, when he was Superior of the Professed House of Goa. He was not consecrated and became Parish Priest of Salsette in 1677 and Provincial of Goa (1677–80) and died on 12 December, 1688.

He wrote a *Life of Brother Pedro de Basto* and in the course of his researches in connection with this biography he became greatly interested in Ceylon about which the Brother had had many visions. He therefore investigated the history of Ceylon and decided to write a book on it and wrote (1671—1688) "*The Temporal and Spiritual Conquest of Ceylon.*" The manuscript was sent to Lisbon for publication, but was not printed and found its way to the Royal Library. Don Joao IV took this library to Brazil during the Napoleonic wars and left the manuscript of Queyroz to the National Library of Rio. A copy made for the Instituto Historico e Georaphico of Brazil in 1840 was entered in the Catalogue and mentioned by Sommervogel. This led Mgr. Ladislaus Zaleski, the Papal Delegate in Ceylon, to procure a copy, which he used for his work entitled *Le Christianisme á Ceylan*. The copy of Mgr. Zaleski was gifted to the Papal Seminary Kandy, where Dr. P. E. Pieris saw it. Realizing its value Dr. Pieris succeeded in purchasing the 1840 copy of Brazil and published translated extracts of the *Conquista* in a book printed over his name under the title of *Ceylon, the Portuguese Era*.

When Dr. Pieris in his turn was going to dispose of the manuscript, the existence of which was so far guarded a secret, the Government intervened and bought the manuscript. After an attempt to get the Hakluyt Society to publish the text and a translation, the Government invited Dr. Pieris to do so. He declined the offer and the Government printed the Portuguese text at the Government Printing Press under the superintendence of Dr. Pieris.

When the book was issued I reviewed it in the *Ceylon Antiquary and Literary Register* pointing out the manner in which it had been used in the *Portuguese Era*. The Government, thereupon, invited me to translate the work, which I did.

"The Temporal and Spiritual Conquest of Ceylon
by
Father Fernao de Queyroz,
of the Society of Jesus,
sometime Provincial of Goa,
Translated by Father S. G. Perera
of the same Society.
Colombo Govt. Press 1930, 3 Vols."

The *Vida do Ven. Ir. Pedro de Basto* was printed at Lisbon in 1689. About another work of Father Queyroz see *Bulletin of the School of Oriental Studies* V. ii (1929)

12. ROIZ, MANOEL, (1551–1623) born at Villaviciosa, Evora, joined the Society in 1579 and arrived in India in 1597. He was at San Thome in 1602, Rector of Cochin in 1606, Visitator of Malacca 1610–11, Rector of Colombo, 1617-1619, Socius of the Visitator 1619, and finally Provincial of Malabar, 1622–1623, when he died on 18 June. He wrote several of the Annual Letters. One relating to the 'Rebellion of Nikapitiya' in 1617 and to the 'Treaty of Peace between the Portuguese and the King of Kandy' which he discussed as a member of the General's Council, was published in the *Ceylon Antiquary* under the title of "Historical Records of the Society of Jesus" C. A. II 130-135, III 49-52.

13. RUBINO, ANTONIO, (1578-1643) born at Strambino, Italy, entered the Society of Jesus in 1596 and set out for India in 1610. He was Rector of Meliapore and Cochin and visited Ceylon in 1605 and 1611. In 1619 he was appointed Rector of the College of Colombo, and 1623 Rector of the Fishery Coast, in 1637 Visitator of Japan, in 1640 Rector of Malacca, and was martyred at Nagasaki on 22 March 1643.

He knew Tamil and Telugu and was the author of *Catena Evangelica*, published in 1640. Some of his letters were published along with a Biographical sketch *La Vie et le Martyr des RR. PP. Antonio Rubino*.........Bordeaux 1687. *Vita del* P. A. Rubino, 1894. *Breve Memoria delle Vita del V. P. Giovanni Antonio Rubino* S. J. Torino-1898.

A manuscript work of his (1641) replying to some calumnies against the Jesuits in China, exists in the

Vittorio Emmanuele Library, Rome, (Gesuiti). The manuscript of another work is in the *Bibliotheque National* of Paris.

14. SCHURHAMMER, GEORGE, born 1882, now Professor of Missiology in the Gregorian University, published a number of Ceylon documents in his *Ceylon zur Zeit des Konigs Bhuvaneka Bahu und Frans Xavers* 1539—1552, Leipzig 1928, 2 Vols., and in *Die Zeitgenossischen Quellen zur Geschichte Portugiesisch-Asiens und Seiner Nachbarlander* 1538–1552, Leipzig, 1932.

The Introduction I to the former was printed in an English Translation in *Ceylon Literary Register* IV (1935—6) pp. 379—385, 426—434. The second part of the Introduction: " The History of Ceylon 1539–1552 according to the hitherto existing Literature " (64 pages) is a marvellous piece of the most accurate research.

INDEX